The Middle Path to Wealth

OrangeBooks Publication

1st Floor, Rajhans Arcade, Mall Road, Kohka, Bhilai, Chhattisgarh 490020

Website: **www.orangebooks.in**

First Edition, 2026

ISBN: 978-93-7426-047-0

Price: Rs. 312.00

Printed in India

The Middle Path to Wealth

Buddhist Wisdom for Conscious Wealth and a Meaningful Life

Ramkrishna Jalinder Gaikwad

OrangeBooks Publication

www.orangebooks.in

'अत्त दीपो भव'

Dedication

To my father, Jalinder Gaikwad.

Who taught me that success earned in silence

is louder than applause,

that integrity is the strongest asset,

and that hard work needs no witness.

This book is his legacy—written in my words,

but shaped by his life.

How to Read This Book

This is not a book to rush through.

It was not written to be consumed quickly, skimmed for tips, or treated as a checklist for better returns. It was written to be **experienced**—slowly, honestly, and reflectively.

You may find that this book does not behave like most financial books.

It will not constantly tell you *what to do*.

Instead, it will often ask you *what you notice*.

That is intentional.

Read for Awareness, Not Accumulation

Each chapter explores not only money, but the **mind behind money**—desire, fear, patience, attachment, contentment, responsibility, and impermanence. These themes are cumulative. Their value deepens when given space.

You do not need to agree with everything.

You only need to **pause long enough to observe your own reactions**.

If a chapter makes you uncomfortable, restless, or unusually calm—stay with that feeling. That response is part of the learning.

One Chapter at a Time Is Enough

This book rewards **measured reading**.

One chapter per sitting—or even per week—is sufficient. Many readers will benefit from stopping at the reflection section and returning later. There is no advantage in speed here.

Progress in this book is not measured by pages completed, but by **clarity gained**.

Read as an Investor—and as a Human Being

You may read this book as:

- An investor
- A professional
- A business owner
- A planner for your family

But you are also reading it as a human being navigating uncertainty, responsibility, ambition, and time.

Let both perspectives remain present.

This Is Not About Perfection

You are not expected to become:

- Fearless
- Perfectly disciplined
- Endlessly patient

This book does not ask for ideal behavior.

It asks for **slightly more awareness than before**.

Small shifts in understanding often produce the most durable change.

Return When Life Changes

This is a book you may return to:

- During market volatility
- During career transitions
- During success
- During uncertainty

Different chapters will speak differently at different stages of life. That is not inconsistency. That is relevance.

A Final Invitation

If this book helps you:

- Pause before reacting
- Loosen one unnecessary attachment
- Choose patience over urgency
- Treat money as a support, not a judge

Then it has done its work.

Read it the way wealth is meant to be built:

With patience, intention, and respect for time.

Author Bio

The author is a seasoned financial counselor and practitioner who has been guiding individuals and families toward financial stability and long-term wealth since **2002**. Over more than two decades of hands-on experience, he has worked closely with human behavior across market cycles—booms, crashes, uncertainty, and recovery.

Today, he manages and advises **over 3,000 clients globally**, overseeing approximately **₹500 crore in assets**, while maintaining a disciplined, long-term, and values-driven approach to money. His work goes beyond numbers and returns; it focuses on how people *think, feel, and act* around money.

Through years of observation, the author recognized a recurring truth:

Financial success is rarely limited by income or intelligence, but by **fear, desire, impatience, comparison, and emotional decision-making**. This realization led him to explore deeper philosophical frameworks that address the inner roots of financial behavior.

Drawing inspiration from **Buddhist philosophy**, behavioral finance, and lived professional experience, the author brings a rare blend of **practical financial wisdom and reflective insight**. His writing does not promote shortcuts, speculation, or rigid formulas. Instead, it encourages clarity, balance, patience, ethical earning, and mindful wealth creation.

The Middle Path to Wealth is the culmination of this journey—written not as a technical manual or religious text, but as a guide for anyone seeking financial security **without inner conflict**.

At the heart of his work lies a simple belief:

Money should support life, not dominate it.

Acknowledgements

No book that explores inner clarity and outer responsibility is ever written alone.

My first gratitude is to the thousands of individuals and families who, over the years, entrusted me with their financial lives. Their questions, fears, hopes, mistakes, and resilience became my greatest teachers. Every market cycle, every difficult conversation, and every moment of doubt offered insights no textbook could provide.

I am deeply grateful to my clients across generations and geographies, whose journeys revealed a simple truth again and again: financial challenges are rarely about numbers alone—they are about human behavior, emotions, and meaning.

I acknowledge the quiet influence of Buddhist philosophy, not as a belief system, but as a framework of wisdom that illuminated the patterns I was already witnessing in real life. Its emphasis on balance, impermanence, awareness, and compassion gave language to experiences I had long observed but not fully understood.

My sincere thanks to mentors, colleagues, and fellow professionals who challenged my thinking, encouraged ethical practice, and reminded me that long-term trust matters more than short-term success.

I am grateful to my family for their patience and support throughout this journey—especially for understanding the long silences, the constant reflection, and the many revisions that clarity demands.

Finally, I thank the reader.

If this book encourages even a small pause before a decision,

a little more patience during uncertainty,

or a gentler relationship with money—

then its purpose is fulfilled.

Foreword

There comes a moment in every serious conversation about money when numbers alone are no longer enough.

Not because they lack importance—

but because, on their own, they lack meaning.

Returns can be calculated.

Assets can be measured.

Risk can be modeled.

Yet beneath every financial decision lies something far less visible and far more powerful: **the human mind**.

After years of observing markets, institutions, leaders, investors, and ordinary individuals across cycles of growth and crisis, one truth becomes impossible to ignore—

Money does not merely reflect economic conditions; **it reflects the inner state of those who engage with it**.

Fear disguises itself as caution.

Desire presents itself as ambition.

Attachment pretends to be security.

Impatience calls itself opportunity.

And quietly, these forces shape outcomes far more than spreadsheets ever will.

This book begins where most financial frameworks end: **with awareness**.

The Middle Path to Wealth offers something rare in contemporary financial literature—a thoughtful union of **timeless wisdom and practical realism**.

Drawing from Buddhist philosophy—not as religion, belief, or doctrine, but as a profound understanding of human behavior—the author reminds us of a truth repeatedly confirmed by history: **extremes are destabilizing**.

In markets.

In leadership.

In personal life.

Excess creates fragility.

Deprivation creates resentment.

Both eventually lead to imbalance.

Sustainable success emerges not from swinging between extremes, but from **balance rooted in clarity**.

This is the Middle Path.

Not compromise.

Not mediocrity.

But disciplined wisdom applied consistently over time.

What makes this work particularly compelling is that its philosophy is not theoretical.

The author does not write from abstraction or ideology, but from **lived experience**—from years of closely observing how people actually behave with money: during market euphoria, during periods of fear and panic, and during the long, quiet stretches when discipline matters most and attention fades.

From this vantage point, one insight becomes unmistakably clear:

Wealth without inner stability amplifies anxiety.

Wealth guided by awareness creates resilience.

In leadership terms, this is not spiritual idealism.

It is **sound strategy**.

To earn ethically.

To invest patiently.

To manage risk without illusion.

To grow without destabilizing oneself—or the systems one depends on.

These are not soft values.

They are **enduring principles** that outlast cycles, trends, and headlines.

The spiritual depth of this book lies in its reminder of **impermanence**.

Markets rise and fall.

Careers evolve.

Fortunes change.

Certainty dissolves.

Expecting permanence in an impermanent world is the true source of suffering—financial and otherwise.

The corporate wisdom lies in what follows from that insight:

preparation instead of prediction,

discipline instead of reaction,

long-term thinking instead of urgency.

Together, these perspectives form a framework that is both **humane and effective**—one that respects reality without surrendering to fear.

This is not a book that promises shortcuts, guarantees, or certainty.

Instead, it offers something far more valuable: **equanimity in decision-making**.

It teaches that patience is not passivity.

That restraint is not weakness.

That contentment is not complacency.

It shows how generosity strengthens systems,

how ethical action compounds trust,

and how clarity of intention simplifies complexity.

In an age overwhelmed by noise, this book offers steadiness.

In a culture obsessed with excess, it restores dignity to *enough*.

In a profession driven by speed, it reclaims the quiet power of thoughtfulness.

If you are seeking wealth without losing perspective,

success without inner conflict,

and progress without regret—

this book will meet you where you are.

May it guide not only your financial decisions,

but your relationship with money itself,

so that wealth becomes a support for life,

not a source of pressure.

30 Wisdom Quotes on Buddha's Economic Thought, Guidance & Prosperity

I. On Right Livelihood & Wealth Creation

1. "Wealth is not a sin; the attachment to wealth is the root of suffering."

– Gautama Buddha

2. "Right Livelihood is a way to earn a living without causing harm to others or the environment."

– The Eightfold Path

3. "The wise person accumulates wealth just as a bee collects nectar from flowers, without harming the color or the fragrance."

– Dhammapada

4. "Prosperity is not found in having much, but in needing little."

– Buddhist Wisdom

5. "Earn your living through honest effort and use it for the welfare of your family and society."

– Sigalovada Sutta

II. On Balanced Living & The Middle Path

6. "A balanced life is the foundation of a balanced economy."

   – The Middle Path

7. "Economic growth without inner peace is like a house built on sand."

   – Modern Buddhist Proverb

8. "The Middle Way avoids the extremes of luxury and poverty; it is the path to sustainable stability."

   – Gautama Buddha

9. "Happiness does not come from consuming more, but from being more."

   – E.F. Schumacher

10. "Contentment is the greatest wealth."

    – Dhammapada

III. On Labor & Human Value

11. "Work is not a curse; it is an opportunity to serve and realize one's potential."

    – Buddhist Management

12. "A machine can do the work of fifty ordinary men. No machine can do the work of one extraordinary man with 'Karuna' (Compassion)."

    –Inspired by Zen Wisdom

13. "The value of a human being is not measured by their salary, but by their contribution to the common good."

– Buddhist Economics

14. "Labor should be a source of joy and mindfulness, not a burden of stress."

– Thich Nhat Hanh

15. "When the mind is pure, joy follows like a shadow that never leaves."

– Dhammapada

IV. On Social Justice & Equality

16. "No one is high or low by birth; only by their actions does a person become noble or ignoble."

– Gautama Buddha

17. "An economy that excludes the poor is an economy that fails the soul of humanity."

– Dr. B.R. Ambedkar

18. "True prosperity is shared prosperity."

– Emperor Ashoka's Philosophy

19. "The strength of a nation lies not in its riches, but in how it treats its most vulnerable."

– Buddhist Leadership

20. "Equality is the sunlight in which the flower of democracy blooms."

– Dr. B.R. Ambedkar

V. On Sustainability & Nature

21. "Nature provides enough to satisfy every man's need, but not every man's greed."

– (Based on Buddhist Ecology)

22. "We do not inherit the Earth from our ancestors; we borrow it from our children."

– Sustainability Ethos

23. "A green economy is a compassionate economy."

– Bhutanese GNH Wisdom

24. "Protect the tree that gives you shade; protect the nature that gives you life."

– Buddhist Scripture

25. "Our survival depends on our realization that we are all interconnected."

– Pratityasamutpada (Interdependence)

VI. On Future & Visionary Leadership

26. "A true leader leads by 'Dhamma,' not by 'Danda' (Force)."

– Emperor Ashoka

27. "Invest in the mind, and you invest in the future of the world."

– Buddhist Education

28. "The goal of economics should be the maximum of well-being with the minimum of consumption."

– E.F. Schumacher

29. "Peace is the highest form of prosperity."

– Dhammapada

30. "Be the light to your own economic path; be 'Atta Deepo Bhava.'"

– Gautama Buddha

Table of Contents

PART - I

Foundations of Buddhist Thought (Philosophy Core)

Chapter - 1
The Middle Path: Balance over Extremes

Why Financial Wisdom Begins with Equilibrium

Where Inner Stillness Meets Financial Intelligence

Why Sustainable Wealth Begins with Balance

The first lesson of wisdom did not arise from theory.

It arose from experience.

When Gautama Buddha reflected on his life before awakening, he recognized a clear pattern.

Luxury distracted the mind.

Deprivation distorted it.

One weakened awareness through indulgence.

The other hardened awareness through denial.

Neither produced truth.

Neither produced freedom.

Clarity emerged only when both extremes were abandoned.

This realization came to be known as **the Middle Path**—not a compromise, but a higher intelligence. A way of living grounded in balance, realism, awareness, and sustainability.

In modern financial life, this wisdom is not symbolic.

It is **operational**.

Most financial stress does not originate from insufficient income.

It arises from **imbalanced behavior, emotional attachment, and reactive decision-making**.

Money: A Tool, an Energy, a Responsibility

From a spiritual perspective, money is neutral energy—a means, not meaning.

From a corporate perspective, money is capital—a resource that must be allocated intelligently.

Problems arise when money becomes:

- Identity instead of utility
- Fear instead of preparation
- Ambition without discipline
- Restraint without purpose

Spiritual imbalance creates anxiety.

Financial imbalance creates fragility.

The Middle Path aligns **inner awareness with external structure**. It allows us to:

- Grow wealth without obsession

- Manage risk without paralysis
- Enjoy comfort without guilt
- Pursue ambition without exhaustion

Balance is not moral restraint.

It is **clarity in action**.

Financial Extremes: Where Suffering Enters

The Extreme of Excess (Attachment)

This extreme is driven by desire, validation, and comparison:

- Lifestyle inflation disconnected from cash-flow strength
- Spending to signal success rather than support life
- Chasing high returns without understanding risk
- Concentration driven by stories, not strategy
- Self-worth measured through possessions

Spiritually, this is attachment.

Financially, this is unmanaged risk.

It leads to:

- Higher fixed obligations
- Emotional dependence on markets
- Vulnerability during downturns

The Extreme of Fear (Aversion)

This extreme is driven by insecurity and uncertainty:

- Hoarding cash beyond reasonable liquidity needs
- Avoiding equity despite long-term goals
- Postponing decisions indefinitely
- Denying comfort despite adequate means
- Viewing money only as protection

Spiritually, this is fear.

Financially, this is opportunity loss.

It results in:

- Erosion of purchasing power
- Stagnation of capital
- Silent, long-term regret

Both extremes interrupt compounding.

Both disturb inner peace.

The Middle Path avoids **both attachment and aversion**.

Balance Is Not Moderation — It Is Right Measure

Balance does not mean equal spending and saving.

It does not mean diluted ambition or average outcomes.

Balance means:

- Spending aligned with dignity, health, and values

- Saving structured for uncertainty, not anxiety
- Investing aligned with time horizon and objectives
- Risk taken consciously, not emotionally
- Enjoyment permitted within defined boundaries

Spiritually, balance is **non-attachment with engagement**.

Corporately, balance is **risk-adjusted decision-making**.

The Middle Path replaces impulse with process,

reaction with structure,

emotion with awareness.

Story: Ramesh — From Oscillation to Equilibrium

Ramesh was a capable professional. His income rose steadily and his career progressed.

Early in life, he lived simply. Savings were consistent. Investments were disciplined. Peace existed.

As income increased, expectations followed. Colleagues upgraded homes. Friends displayed success online. Status became visible—and contagious.

Gradually:

- Housing costs increased
- Discretionary spending expanded
- Fixed obligations hardened

Initially, it felt like growth.

Later, it felt like pressure.

Despite higher income, anxiety grew. Market volatility disturbed him. Savings felt inadequate. Sleep suffered.

This was not a financial failure.

It was imbalance through excess.

Reacting to stress, Ramesh swung to the opposite extreme. He cut spending sharply, withdrew socially, avoided investing, and focused only on accumulation.

Cash increased.

Peace did not.

In a quiet conversation, a senior colleague said:

"Money should reduce your worries—not replace them."

That sentence shifted something deeper than strategy.

Ramesh realized he had never stabilized—he had only oscillated.

Instead of reacting, he recalibrated:

- Separated needs from ego-driven expenses
- Restored systematic investing
- Built buffers, not rigid walls
- Allowed measured enjoyment

Nothing dramatic changed.

Yet everything stabilized.

Income remained the same.

Peace returned.

Because **balance returned**.

Why the Middle Path Builds Enduring Wealth

Spiritually:

- Balance reduces inner turbulence
- Awareness replaces anxiety
- Contentment replaces comparison

Corporately:

- Disciplined allocation survives volatility
- Diversification absorbs shocks
- Compounding rewards consistency
- Emotional control preserves capital

Markets do not consistently reward brilliance.

They reward **repeatable discipline**.

Life does not sustain extremes.

It sustains balance lived over time.

The Middle Path transforms money:

- From fear → into a support system
- From status → into stability
- From emotional weight → into quiet strength

Inner Wealth and Outer Wealth

Outer wealth is what you accumulate.

Inner wealth is what you are not afraid of losing.

When money is handled with balance:

- Decisions Become Calmer
- Sleep Deepens
- Relationships Soften
- Perspective Returns

True prosperity is not aggressive expansion.

It is **freedom from constant disturbance**.

Balance creates space—for thinking, for living, for meaning.

Investor Reflection – Chapter 1

Most long-term investment failures are not caused by lack of opportunity.

They are caused by **extremes in behavior**.

On one side are investors who chase returns aggressively—overexposed to a single asset, strategy, or narrative.

On the other side are investors who remain overly conservative—holding excessive cash, avoiding equity, and postponing decisions indefinitely.

Both extremes feel justified.

Both destroy balance.

Markets reward neither excitement nor fear.

They reward **repeatable discipline**.

Balanced investors:

- Allocate risk consciously, not emotionally
- Grow wealth without turning it into identity
- Prepare for volatility instead of reacting to it
- Allow enjoyment without guilt and ambition without anxiety

In professional investing, balance appears as:

- Diversification instead of story-driven concentration
- Asset allocation instead of prediction
- Patience instead of urgency

The Middle Path does not eliminate risk.

It manages risk **without disturbing the mind**.

An investor who avoids extremes may appear unremarkable in any single year—but over time, such investors quietly outperform those who oscillate between enthusiasm and fear.

Quiet balance compounds.

Extremes interrupt.

Chapter Takeaway

The Middle Path is not cautious living.

It is **intelligent, conscious, professional living**.

Money managed without extremes does not announce success.

It quietly sustains it—year after year.

Reflection Exercises – Chapter 1

1. Awareness Audit

Where in my financial life am I driven by attachment or fear?

2. Alignment Check

Which financial habits reflect ego, anxiety, or imitation rather than intention?

3. Structural Balance

One area where structure can replace reaction (spending, investing, saving).

4. Emotional Insight

Which emotion dominates my money decisions most often?

5. One Conscious Commitment

One small, balanced action I will take this month—without extremes.

Chapter - 2
The Four Noble Truths & Money Suffering

Why Financial Stress Is Universal — and How Freedom Is Possible

Where Honest Awareness Becomes Lasting Stability

Wisdom does not begin with solutions.

It begins with **truthful observation**.

This is why Gautama Buddha did not start his teaching with techniques, discipline, or hope. He began with a fact so simple, yet so uncomfortable, that it could not be denied:

Suffering exists.

Centuries later, in a world of rising incomes, complex investment products, and endless financial advice, this truth remains profoundly relevant.

Financial suffering exists.

It is widespread.

And it is often invisible.

This chapter explores the **Four Noble Truths** not as religious doctrine, but as a clear, practical framework to understand money-related stress, anxiety, and freedom—both **spiritually and professionally**.

The Honest Beginning: Acknowledging Financial Suffering

Financial suffering does not look the same for everyone.

It may appear as:

- Persistent anxiety about the future
- Stress during market volatility
- Dissatisfaction despite rising income
- Fear of loss even after success
- Pressure to maintain a lifestyle
- Constant mental noise around money

This suffering is not limited to those who lack money.

It affects:

- Professionals with steady salaries
- Entrepreneurs with growing businesses
- Investors with diversified portfolios
- Retirees with adequate assets

Spiritually, this suffering is **dukkha**—unease, restlessness, dissatisfaction.

Corporately, it is **emotional risk**—an invisible drag on judgment and decision-making.

Financial stress is not a personal failure.

It is a **human condition**.

Ignoring it does not remove it.

Understanding it transforms it.

The First Noble Truth: Financial Suffering Exists

Modern society encourages appearances.

Stability is displayed.

Anxiety is concealed.

Behind confident profiles and comfortable lives, many quietly experience:

- Constant comparison with others
- Pressure to keep upgrading
- Worry about uncertainty
- Confusion about *"how much is enough"*

The First Noble Truth does not judge this experience.

It simply **recognizes** it.

Recognition is not weakness.

Spiritually, it is awareness.

Professionally, it is problem definition.

No strategy—financial or personal—works without clarity.

The Second Noble Truth: The Cause of Financial Suffering

The Buddha identified the root of suffering as **Tanha**—craving and attachment.

In financial life, this craving takes subtle, socially accepted forms:

- The desire for more even when needs are met
- Attachment to status, comparison, and image
- Obsession with certainty in an uncertain world
- Fear-driven clinging to outcomes and numbers

Slowly, money changes its role:

- From *tool → to identity*
- From *resource → to security*
- From *utility → to validation*

When wealth carries identity, every fluctuation feels personal.

Markets stop being movements.

They become judgments.

Spiritually, this is **attachment**.

Corporately, this is **behavioral bias**.

This is the hidden engine of financial suffering.

Story: Meera and the Invisible Pressure

Meera appeared financially successful by every visible measure.

She earned well.

She invested regularly.

She avoided unnecessary debt.

Friends described her as "sorted."

Yet peace eluded her.

Market corrections unsettled her deeply. Headlines dictated her mood. She checked her portfolio repeatedly—not to act, but to reassure herself.

One evening, in a quiet conversation with her mother, Meera admitted:

"I have enough, yet I'm always tense."

Her mother replied gently:

"Then maybe the problem isn't money.

Maybe it's the fear of losing what money represents."

That moment reframed everything.

Meera's anxiety did not come from lack.

It came from **attachment**.

Her sense of safety depended on numbers remaining constant—

In a world defined by change.

The Second Noble Truth explained her suffering **without blame**.

The Third Noble Truth: Freedom Is Possible

Buddhism does not end with diagnosis.

It offers **liberation**.

If craving causes suffering,

then reducing craving reduces suffering.

This does not mean rejecting money, ambition, or growth.

It means releasing the belief that money can provide permanent certainty or identity.

True financial freedom is not a number.

It is the ability to:

- Face volatility without panic
- Make decisions without fear
- Accept uncertainty without paralysis
- Separate self-worth from net worth

Spiritually, this is **non-attachment**.

Corporately, this is **emotional resilience**.

Peace often appears **before** circumstances change.

The Fourth Noble Truth: A Practical Path Forward

The Buddha outlined the Eightfold Path as a way out of suffering.

Applied to money, it becomes a framework for conscious, disciplined financial living.

- **Right Understanding**

  Markets are uncertain by nature. Volatility is normal, not failure.

- **Right Intention**

  Wealth for stability, dignity, and meaning—not ego or comparison.

- **Right Action**

  Ethical earning, disciplined spending, responsible investing.

- **Right Effort**

  Consistency over shortcuts. Process over prediction.

- **Right Mindfulness**

  Awareness of emotions during spending, saving, and investing.

This path does not promise extraordinary returns.

It promises **clarity, resilience, and endurance**.

Money as a Mirror, Not a Villain

Money does not create suffering.

It reveals what already exists:

- Fear
- Desire
- Insecurity
- Comparison

Handled unconsciously, money amplifies confusion.

Handled mindfully, money becomes a teacher.

Spiritually, it exposes attachment.

Financially, it exposes behavioral patterns.

The Four Noble Truths do not eliminate financial challenges.

They transform our relationship with them.

Investor Reflection – Chapter 2

Financial stress is often misunderstood as a technical problem.

In reality, it is a **behavioral and emotional condition**.

Many investors experience anxiety even when portfolios are well-constructed and goals are realistic. This suffering does not arise from markets alone—it arises from attachment, expectation, and craving for certainty.

Investors suffer when:

- Returns are expected to be smooth
- Volatility is treated as failure
- Money becomes identity or security

The Four Noble Truths offer a clear investor insight:

Suffering exists, it has causes, it can be reduced, and there is a path forward.

Professionally, that path is not prediction—it is **preparation**.

Investors who accept uncertainty:

- Stay invested during volatility
- Avoid panic-driven exits
- Make decisions from process, not emotion

Markets will never remove uncertainty.

But understanding its nature removes unnecessary suffering.

The calm investor is not the one with the highest return in any single year—

but the one who remains emotionally stable across cycles.

Chapter Takeaway

Financial suffering is not accidental.

It arises from craving and attachment.

Freedom does not come from eliminating uncertainty.

It comes from **understanding it**.

Wealth grows faster with discipline.

Peace grows faster with awareness.

Reflection Exercises – Chapter 2

1. **Awareness Check**

Which financial situations create the most stress for me right now?

2. **Reality Test**

Is my anxiety driven by real need—or imagined fear?

3. **Belief Mapping**

One belief about money that may be increasing my suffering.

4. **Emotional Insight**

Which emotion dominates my financial life most often—fear, craving, or comparison?

5. **One Conscious Shift**

One small step this month to reduce attachment and restore balance.

Chapter - 3
Desire (Tanha) vs. Need

How craving silently shapes spending, lifestyle inflation, and dissatisfaction

The Quiet Engine behind Most Financial Decisions

Very few financial problems begin with insufficient income.

Most begin with **unexamined desire**.

In Buddhist philosophy, *Tanha* is not ordinary wanting. It is a restless craving that believes fulfillment lies just beyond the next acquisition. Tanha does not shout. It persuades. It rarely announces itself as greed. It arrives as **justification**.

Needs are limited and honest.

Desires are adaptive and endless.

This distinction explains one of the great paradoxes of modern life:

People earn more than ever before, yet feel increasingly dissatisfied.

How Desire Disguises Itself as Necessity

Desire is rarely reckless.

It is articulate.

It sounds reasonable.

It says:

- “I’ve earned this.”
- “This is required at my level.”
- “Everyone around me has upgraded.”
- “This will improve my quality of life.”

Over time, desire quietly **redefines normal**.

What was once optional becomes essential.

What was once luxury becomes baseline.

What was once enough becomes insufficient.

This gradual psychological shift forms the foundation of **lifestyle inflation**—not dramatic overspending, but *normalized excess* that feels invisible while it is happening.

Needs Create Stability; Desire Creates Drift

Needs support life.

Desire constantly moves the finish line.

Needs relate to dignity and well-being:

- Shelter, safety, and health
- Basic comfort
- Education and mobility

Desire relates to identity:

- Status and recognition
- Comparison and validation
- Emotional relief and reassurance

When financial decisions are guided by needs, life stabilizes.

When guided by desire, life accelerates—but rarely settles.

Desire does not destroy finances immediately.

It **erodes clarity slowly**.

Story: Amit and the Moving Baseline

Amit began his career with discipline. He saved regularly, invested consistently, and lived simply. Peace existed alongside progress.

As promotions arrived, life expanded.

A better apartment felt practical.

A premium car felt justified.

Dining out, gadgets, and travel felt like rewards for effort.

Nothing felt irresponsible.

Everything felt earned.

Yet something subtle changed.

Despite higher income, Amit's savings rate stagnated. Market fluctuations began to disturb him. Unexpected expenses felt heavier than before.

One evening, while reviewing his finances, Amit noticed a pattern:

Every increase in income had been absorbed by lifestyle upgrades. His baseline had moved.

He asked himself a difficult question:

"If my income has grown so much, why hasn't my peace?"

The answer was uncomfortable—but clear.

He was no longer chasing needs.

He was feeding **Tanha**—quietly, consistently.

Amit did not impose harsh restrictions. He introduced **awareness**. He paused before upgrades, separated value from validation, and redirected growth toward savings and long-term goals.

Pressure reduced—not because income changed,

but because desire was **observed**.

Lifestyle Inflation: The Hidden Tax on Progress

Lifestyle inflation feels harmless because it is gradual.

Its long-term costs include:

- Reduced saving capacity
- Dependence on continuous income growth
- Intolerance to uncertainty
- Delayed financial freedom

The tragedy is not enjoyment.

It is **loss of choice**.

When desire consumes growth, freedom is postponed indefinitely.

Why Desire Produces Dissatisfaction

Desire operates on a treadmill:

- Satisfaction is brief
- Comparison is constant
- Expectations escalate

The mind adapts quickly to improvement. What once delighted becomes ordinary. What once felt abundant becomes average.

This is why:

- Higher income does not guarantee contentment
- Luxury does not eliminate anxiety
- Success does not silence comparison

Desire multiplies wants faster than income can satisfy them.

The Buddhist Insight: Sufficiency as Liberation

Buddhism introduces **sufficiency** not as limitation, but as freedom.

Sufficiency means:

- Recognizing when needs are met
- Identifying when desire is speaking

- Choosing stability over expansion when necessary

It does not deny pleasure.

It denies **blind pursuit**.

When sufficiency guides decisions:

- Savings grow naturally
- Generosity becomes possible
- Anxiety weakens
- Clarity strengthens

Sufficiency restores sovereignty over choice.

Practical Discernment: Separating Need from Desire

Before significant spending, pause and ask:

- Does this solve a real problem—or create a new obligation?
- Will this increase flexibility—or reduce it?
- If income paused for a year, would this still feel wise?
- Am I buying value—or emotional relief?

Desire demands speed.

Wisdom allows pause.

That pause restores choice.

Investor Reflection – Chapter 3

Many investment decisions that appear rational are quietly driven by desire rather than necessity.

Desire shows up in investing as:

- Chasing returns beyond what goals require
- Increasing risk because "others are doing better"
- Upgrading portfolios for excitement, not alignment
- Confusing lifestyle aspiration with financial need

Needs are finite.

Desire has no finish line.

Investors who fail to separate the two often experience:

- Lifestyle inflation that absorbs surplus income
- Pressure to earn higher returns just to maintain comfort
- Reduced tolerance for volatility
- Delayed financial freedom

Professional investors understand that **sufficient return is more important than maximum return**.

When goals are met, excess risk is not ambition—it is vulnerability.

Desire-driven investing increases emotional noise.

Need-based investing increases clarity.

The disciplined investor regularly asks:

"Does this decision support my long-term life—or merely my short-term excitement?"

Wealth grows faster when desire is **observed**, not obeyed.

Chapter Takeaway

Needs support life.

Desire consumes attention.

Unchecked desire does not make one poor—

it makes one **perpetually unsatisfied**.

Wealth grows faster when desire is disciplined.

Peace grows faster when desire is understood.

Reflection Exercises – Chapter 3

1. Awareness Check

Where has desire quietly replaced need in my lifestyle?

2. Personal Inventory

Which expenses once felt optional but now feel necessary?

3. Behavior Mapping

One purchase or upgrade I can pause or delay this month.

4. Emotional Insight

Which emotion most often triggers my spending—stress, boredom, or comparison?

5. One Quiet Commitment

One desire I will observe without immediately acting on it.

PART - II
Mind, Karma & Financial Behavior

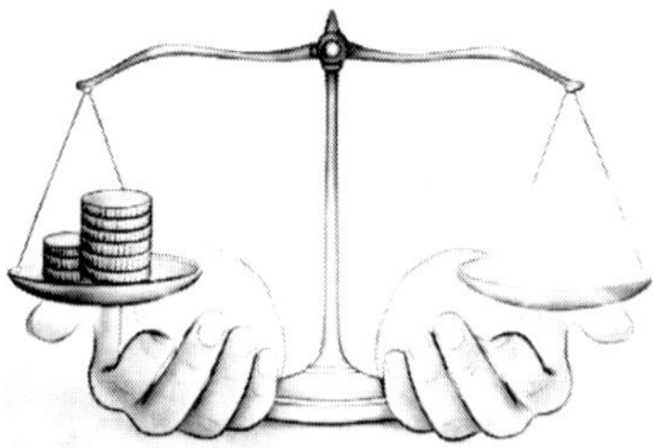

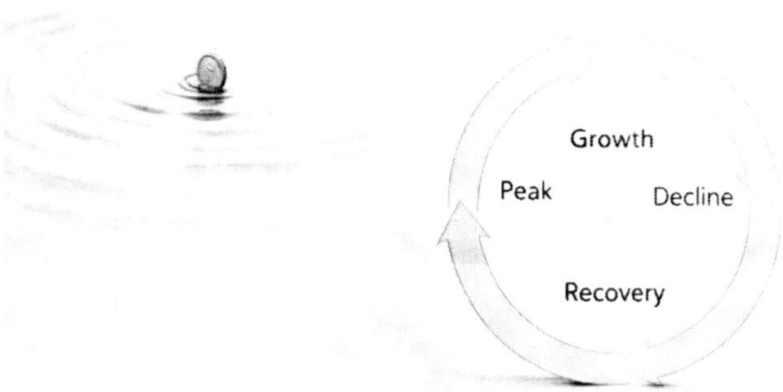
Growth
Peak
Decline
Recovery

Chapter - 4
Karma: Every Financial Action Has Consequences

Why short-term choices quietly shape long-term outcomes

Why Karma Is Not Fate, but Continuity

How Repeated Money Decisions Shape Wealth, Character, and Peace

Karma is one of the most misunderstood ideas in both spiritual and financial life.

It is often mistaken for destiny.

Or punishment.

Or reward handed down by some external force.

In Buddhist philosophy, karma is far simpler—and far more powerful.

Karma means action.

And the consequences that follow.

Nothing mystical.

Nothing moralistic.

Every intention leads to action.

Every action leaves a trace.

Over time, those traces form patterns.

And patterns—repeated long enough—become outcomes.

Why Money Decisions Carry Powerful Karma

Money decisions are among the most **frequent and repetitive actions** in modern life.

- How you spend
- How you save
- How you invest
- How you react to volatility
- How you treat success and loss

Because they are repeated so often, their impact is deeper than rare, dramatic events.

Financial karma is not created by one big mistake or one lucky win.

It is created by **what you do again and again**.

This is why financial outcomes often appear mysterious or unfair.

But they are rarely accidental.

Financial karma is not about luck.

It is about behavior practiced consistently.

Why Consequences Are Often Invisible at First

One reason karma is misunderstood is that consequences are **delayed**.

Many financial choices feel harmless in isolation:

- A small shortcut
- A speculative bet
- A postponed decision
- A compromised value

Sometimes, the immediate result is even positive.

This creates false confidence.

But karma does not operate on immediacy.

It operates on **accumulation**.

The consequence appears later:

- As anxiety
- As instability
- As loss of discipline
- As erosion of trust
- As reduced tolerance for uncertainty

Karma rarely announces itself loudly.

It does not arrive with drama.

It accumulates quietly.

The Three Layers of Financial Consequence

Every financial action affects three dimensions simultaneously—whether we notice it or not.

1. **External Results**
    - Income
    - Returns
    - Losses
    - Net worth

This is the most visible layer—and the one most people focus on.

2. **Relational Impact**
    - Trust with partners and family
    - Reputation with clients and colleagues
    - Dependency on income or markets

This layer determines how much support surrounds you during stress.

3. **Inner Conditioning**
    - Habits
    - Emotional tolerance
    - Patience or restlessness
    - Self-respect and integrity

This third layer is the most powerful—and the most ignored.

Money trains the mind.

What you repeat becomes normal.

What becomes normal becomes character.

And character shapes destiny far more than events.

Story: Sanjay and the Shortcut Habit

Sanjay was intelligent, ambitious, and impatient.

He disliked slow progress.

Long-term investing felt boring.

Steady compounding felt unimpressive.

When a speculative opportunity promised quick gains, he took it—despite weak fundamentals.

The profit arrived fast.

Encouraged, he repeated the behavior.

Gradually, something subtle changed:

- Steady investments felt dull
- Patience felt uncomfortable
- Discipline weakened
- Risk appetite increased

Then, inevitably, one decision went wrong.

The financial loss was manageable.

But the mental cost was heavy.

Sanjay realized something important:

"I didn't just lose money.

I trained myself to expect speed."

The real loss was not capital.

It was the **habit** he had cultivated.

Karma had worked—not as punishment,

but as **continuity**.

Ethical Action as Long-Term Stability

Buddhism emphasizes **Right Action**—acting without causing harm.

In financial life, this translates into:

- Transparency over manipulation
- Sustainability over exploitation
- Long-term trust over short-term gain

Ethical choices may not maximize immediate profit.

But they maximize **durability**.

Trust compounds.

Reputation compounds.

Self-respect compounds.

Unethical gains also compound—

into fear, vigilance, and fragility.

A life built on shortcuts requires constant defense.

A life built on integrity allows ease.

Market Karma: Behavior Repeats Outcomes

Markets do not reward intelligence alone.

They reward behavior under pressure.

- Panic selling locks losses
- Overconfidence invites correction
- Discipline survives cycles

- Patience enables compounding

What often feels like "bad luck" is actually behavior repeated under stress.

Markets are not emotional.

Investors are.

Karma reveals itself most clearly during volatility—

When habits take over and thinking stops.

Karma Shapes Identity before It Shapes Wealth

Over time:

- Disciplined actions create calm investors
- Careless actions create anxious ones
- Ethical earning creates inner alignment
- Shortcuts create inner conflict

Your portfolio fluctuates.

Your habits accumulate.

And habits, eventually, decide both wealth and peace.

Investor Reflection – Chapter 4

In investing, outcomes are often mistaken for luck.

In reality, most outcomes are the result of **repeated behavior**.

Every financial action—however small—trains the investor's mind.

Shortcuts taken once become habits.

Discipline practiced consistently becomes identity.

Long-term investment results are shaped by:

- How investors react to volatility
- How often they interrupt compounding
- How they treat success and failure

Speculative success may deliver quick rewards, but it conditions the mind to expect speed. When markets slow or reverse, that conditioning becomes dangerous.

Professionally successful investors are not those who never make mistakes—

but those who **do not repeat emotional mistakes**.

Ethical behavior, patience, and transparency compound in ways that returns alone cannot:

- Trust strengthens
- Confidence stabilizes
- Decision-making improves

Market karma is simple:

What you repeat under pressure becomes your future behavior.

Wealth built through awareness strengthens resilience.

Wealth built through shortcuts demands repayment later—often with interest.

Chapter Takeaway

Karma does not judge.

It records.

Every financial action trains the mind

and prepares future outcomes.

Wealth built with awareness strengthens life.

Wealth built with shortcuts demands repayment—eventually.

Reflection Exercises – Chapter 4

1. **Awareness Check**

Which financial habits do I repeat most often—positive or negative?

2. **Personal Inventory**

Where have short-term choices created long-term discomfort?

3. **Behavior Mapping**

One habit I can change to improve my future financial outcomes.

4. **Emotional Insight**

When do I feel tempted to take shortcuts—and why?

5. **One Quiet Commitment**

One action I will repeat consistently, regardless of immediate results.

Chapter - 5
Right Livelihood & Ethical Income

Why how you earn matters as much as how much you earn

Income Is Never Neutral

Income is often treated as separate from values.

Work is work. Money is money.

Buddhist philosophy gently—and firmly—disagrees.

It introduces **Right Livelihood** (*Sammā Ājīva*), a principle that asks a deeper and more uncomfortable question:

Does the way you earn reduce suffering—or increase it?

Right Livelihood does not judge wealth by size, status, or appearance.

It examines something far more subtle and enduring:

- **Source** – How is this income generated?
- **Intention** – What motivates the action behind it?
- **Impact** – Who benefits, and who bears the cost?

Money is not morally charged in itself.

But it is never energetically empty.

Money carries the **imprint of how it was earned**.

Income generated with clarity, honesty, and restraint strengthens inner stability.

Income generated through harm, manipulation, or chronic compromise weakens peace—often slowly, quietly, and invisibly at first.

Why Ethical Income Creates Emotional Stability

Financial stress is frequently misunderstood as a numerical problem.

In reality, it is often an **inner conflict**.

When income clashes with conscience:

- Decisions feel heavier
- Justifications become routine
- Anxiety increases without clear cause
- Self-trust quietly erodes

The mind begins to work harder—not on growth, but on rationalization.

Ethical income simplifies life.

There is less to defend.

Less to hide.

Less to fear.

When actions and values align, energy that was once spent managing discomfort becomes available for clarity, creativity, and long-term thinking. Trust—both **internal** and **external**—emerges as a durable asset.

Right Livelihood is not about moral perfection.

It is about **alignment**.

Story: Neha and the Cost of Compromise

Neha worked in a high-pressure sales environment.

The incentives were attractive.

The targets were aggressive.

And subtle pressure to oversell was normalized.

At first, Neha performed well.

Income grew. Recognition followed. Confidence rose.

Gradually, discomfort appeared.

She rehearsed explanations before client calls.

She avoided certain conversations.

She justified half-truths as *"industry practice."*

Nothing she did was illegal.

Yet something felt off.

One day, a long-term client questioned a recommendation she had made months earlier. It wasn't technically wrong—but it wasn't fully honest either.

That conversation lingered.

Weeks later, Neha chose to move into a role with slower income growth but clearer alignment. Her earnings dipped briefly.

Her sleep improved immediately.

Later, she reflected:

"I wasn't exhausted by work.

I was exhausted by compromise."

Right Livelihood restored her energy—not by increasing pay, but by **removing inner conflict**.

Right Livelihood in the Modern Economy

Harm today is rarely obvious.

It is often **indirect**, embedded in systems, incentives, and normalization.

Right Livelihood in the modern world means asking uncomfortable but essential questions:

- Does my work rely on misinformation or fear?
- Does it reward short-term extraction over long-term value?
- Does success depend on others' confusion, pressure, or loss?

Not every system is pure.

The aim is not withdrawal from economic life.

The aim is **conscious participation**.

Even within imperfect structures, intention matters.

Restraint matters.

Choice matters.

Small acts of clarity within flawed systems still reduce suffering.

Ethics as a Compounding Asset:

Ethical income compounds—quietly and powerfully.

- Credibility attracts opportunity

- Trust survives downturns
- Relationships endure pressure
- Inner confidence grows

Unethical income compounds too—but in the opposite direction:

- Vigilance replaces ease
- Instability replaces trust
- Fear of exposure replaces confidence

Over time, the second becomes expensive—not always financially, but psychologically.

Right Livelihood may not maximize short-term income.

It **optimizes sustainability**.

Practical Alignment: Small Corrections Matter

Right Livelihood is rarely achieved through dramatic change.

It is built through **small, consistent corrections**.

You do not need to change careers overnight.

You can:

- Increase transparency where possible
- Reduce pressure-based tactics
- Refuse practices that violate core values
- Choose trust over quick wins

Small choices, repeated over time, reshape trajectory.

Alignment grows quietly—just like peace.

Investor Reflection – Chapter 5

Right Livelihood & Ethical Income

How money is earned quietly shapes how it is experienced.

Investors who earn income aligned with their values tend to:

- Make clearer financial decisions
- Experience less inner conflict
- Tolerate volatility with greater calm

When income is earned through constant compromise, pressure increases. Decisions become defensive. Fear of loss intensifies—not because of numbers, but because **alignment is missing**.

Ethical income is not about moral superiority.

It is about **emotional stability**.

Professionally, trust is a compounding asset.

Reputation reduces friction.

Transparency reduces anxiety.

Investors who build wealth without harming others:

- Sleep better during uncertainty
- Commit to long-term decisions with confidence
- Feel less temptation toward reckless opportunities

Money earned with dignity feels lighter to hold.

Money earned with compromise demands constant vigilance.

In the long run, **alignment is more valuable than acceleration**.

Chapter Takeaway

Right Livelihood is not about earning less.

It is about earning **without erosion**.

Money earned with clarity strengthens life.

Money earned with compromise slowly weakens it.

Reflection Exercises – Chapter 5

1. Awareness Check

Do I feel comfortable explaining how I earn my income?

2. Personal Inventory

Where do I regularly justify discomfort as "normal"?

3. Behavior Mapping

One small ethical correction I can make in my work this month.

4. Emotional Insight

What emotion arises when values and incentives conflict?

5. One Quiet Commitment

One decision I will make that prioritizes alignment over speed.

Chapter - 6
Impermanence (Anicca) & Market Cycles

Why nothing lasts—and why that truth protects investors

The One Law Markets Never Break

In Buddhist philosophy, **Anicca—impermanence**—is not a pessimistic idea.

It is a stabilizing truth.

Everything that arises will change.

Everything that grows will decline.

Everything that falls will eventually rise again.

This is not a belief.

It is an observation.

Suffering does not come from change itself.

It comes from **expecting permanence in an impermanent world**.

Financial markets reflect Anicca with ruthless honesty. Prices move. Cycles repeat. Conditions shift. Yet investors repeatedly behave as if the present environment—good or bad—will last forever.

When markets rise, permanence is assumed.

When markets fall, collapse is assumed.

Both assumptions are incorrect.

Markets do not promise stability.

They promise **movement**.

Why the Mind Resists Impermanence

The human mind craves predictability.

Stability feels safe.

Change feels threatening.

This psychological wiring evolved for survival—not for investing.

During rising markets, the mind whispers comforting illusions:

- "This time is different."
- "Growth is permanent."
- "Risk has disappeared."

During falling markets, the mind shouts urgent warnings:

- "It will never recover."
- "I should exit before it gets worse."

- "The system is broken."

Both reactions deny impermanence.

Optimism denies decline.

Fear denies recovery.

Markets, however, deny neither.

They move—regardless of belief.

Story: Rahul and the Illusion of Stability

Rahul began investing during a strong bull phase.

Returns were steady.

Headlines were optimistic.

Every dip felt temporary and harmless.

Confidence grew quickly.

He increased exposure aggressively.

Emergency reserves felt unnecessary.

Long-term plans were built on continued growth.

Then came a correction.

Portfolio values dropped sharply.

Confidence evaporated.

Fear replaced optimism.

Rahul checked prices compulsively.

Sleep suffered.

Decisions felt urgent and emotional.

The shock was not the decline itself.

It was **his reaction to it**.

A senior investor later told him quietly:

"Markets don't betray expectations.

They ignore them."

That sentence stayed with him.

Rahul did not abandon investing.

He **restructured his understanding**.

He adopted:

- Realistic return assumptions
- Emergency reserves
- Disciplined asset allocation

The correction became **instruction**, not trauma.

Impermanence had not harmed him.

Ignoring it had.

Impermanence as Protection, Not Threat

Impermanence frightens only those who deny it.

When change is expected:

- Volatility feels normal
- Patience becomes easier
- Panic reduces
- Resilience increases

Impermanence reminds us of simple truths:

- Bull markets end
- Bear markets pass
- Cycles repeat

Awareness prevents:

- Overconfidence during prosperity
- Despair during decline

Investors who accept impermanence do not demand certainty from markets. They design their lives and portfolios to **withstand change**.

Market Cycles Are Emotional Cycles

Markets do not move only on fundamentals.

They move on **collective emotion** layered on fundamentals.

- Optimism inflates expectations
- Greed accelerates peaks
- Fear deepens declines
- Despair marks bottoms

Prices often overshoot both value and despair because emotions move faster than reality.

Recognizing impermanence creates **distance** from emotional contagion.

You stop asking:

"What will happen next?"

You start asking:

"How should I behave—regardless of what happens next?"

This shift transforms investing from prediction to preparation.

Practical Wisdom from Anicca

Applying impermanence does not require philosophical depth.

It requires structural discipline.

It means:

- Diversifying across assets
- Avoiding leverage driven by recent trends
- Maintaining emergency buffers
- Investing systematically
- Reviewing plans periodically, not reactively

Impermanence does not demand inaction.

It demands **readiness**.

Preparation replaces prediction.

Structure replaces hope.

Investor Reflection – Chapter 6

Impermanence (Anicca) & Market Cycles

Markets do not move in straight lines—and neither do careers, incomes, or economies.

Investors suffer most when they expect stability in a system defined by change.

Impermanence is not a flaw of markets.

It is the market's nature.

Investors who internalize this truth:

- Prepare instead of predict
- Diversify instead of concentrate
- Build buffers instead of relying on optimism

Those who deny impermanence often behave as if:

- Bull markets are permanent
- Bear markets are terminal
- Recent trends will continue indefinitely

This leads to:

- Overconfidence at peaks
- Panic at lows
- Emotional decision-making at exactly the wrong time

Professional investors treat cycles as **normal, not personal**.

They design portfolios to survive change—not to escape it.

When impermanence is accepted:

- Volatility loses emotional power
- Patience becomes practical

- Discipline feels natural

Markets do not punish change.

They punish those who **refuse to plan for it**.

Chapter Takeaway

Impermanence is not a risk.

Ignoring impermanence is.

Those who accept change are rarely surprised.

Those who resist it are repeatedly shaken.

Reflection Exercises – Chapter 6

1. Awareness Check

Where do I assume current financial conditions will continue unchanged?

2. Personal Inventory

How do I emotionally react to market movement—calm, fear, excitement, or denial?

3. Behavior Mapping

One adjustment that would make my financial plan more resilient to change.

4. Emotional Insight

Do fear or overconfidence influence my decisions more?

5. One Quiet Commitment

One way I will prepare for change rather than attempt to predict it.

PART - III
Buddhist Psychology & Personal Finance

Need
Comfort
More
Danger
Self Worth
Peace
Certainty
Status
Awareness

Chapter - 7
Attachment: The Root of Financial Anxiety

Why holding too tightly creates fear

How clinging turns normal fluctuation into emotional suffering

Why Money Feels Heavier Than It Is

Money is neutral. Anxiety is not.

Money becomes heavy not because of its amount, but because of **what we attach to it**.

In Buddhist psychology, attachment (*Upādāna*) is clinging—to outcomes, identities, roles, or possessions—as if they can guarantee lasting security. It is the unconscious belief that *"if this remains stable, I will be safe."*

When money becomes attached to:

- Self-worth
- Personal identity
- Certainty about the future
- Social standing or validation

Fear becomes inevitable.

Because money, by its very nature, **moves**.

Markets fluctuate.

Incomes vary.

Expenses appear unexpectedly.

Attachment turns this natural movement into emotional threat.

Attachment Turns Movement into Threat

Without attachment:

- A market fall is information
- An expense is a situation to manage
- Income variation is an adjustment

With attachment:

- A market fall feels like personal failure
- An expense feels like danger
- Income variation feels like loss of control

Attachment **personalizes uncertainty**.

This is why two people can face the same financial event—

the same market correction, the same expense, the same income change—

and experience completely different emotional outcomes.

The difference is not money.

It is **entanglement**.

Story: Kavita and the Habit of Constant Checking

Kavita was financially disciplined.

She saved regularly.

She invested prudently.

She avoided unnecessary debt.

On paper, everything was in order.

Yet she was anxious.

She checked her portfolio multiple times a day.

News headlines dictated her mood.

Small market movements disturbed her sleep.

Objectively, nothing in her plan required action.

One evening, she asked herself a simple but unsettling question:

"If my strategy hasn't changed, why has my peace?"

The answer became clear.

Her sense of safety was attached to **numbers staying stable**.

Volatility felt like threat—not movement.

Kavita began practicing distance, not denial:

- Checking investments less frequently
- Reviewing performance periodically, not daily
- Focusing on behavior rather than outcomes

Over time, anxiety reduced—not because markets became calm,

but because **attachment loosened**.

Her plan did not change.

Her relationship with uncertainty did.

The Illusion of Control

Attachment often disguises itself as control.

It looks like:

- Constant monitoring
- Excessive reassurance
- Over-planning for every scenario
- Intolerance of uncertainty

But control over outcomes is an illusion.

Markets will fluctuate.

Returns will vary.

Life will interrupt plans.

What we truly control is:

- Saving behavior
- Investment discipline
- Response to volatility
- Adherence to long-term process

Attachment exhausts energy trying to control what cannot be fixed.

Detachment conserves energy by focusing on what **can** be guided.

Detachment Is Not Neglect

Detachment is often misunderstood.

It does not mean indifference.

It does not mean irresponsibility.

It does not mean disengagement.

Detachment means **engagement without obsession**.

- You invest—but don't panic
- You earn—but don't cling
- You plan—but don't demand certainty

Detachment replaces anxiety with flexibility.

Ironically, investors who are less attached often perform better—

not because they care less, but because they make **fewer emotional mistakes**.

Attachment and Loss Aversion

Behavioral finance confirms what Buddhism observed centuries ago:

Humans fear losses more than they value equivalent gains.

Attachment amplifies this bias.

When identity is tied to wealth:

- Losses feel personal

- Decisions become reactive
- Long-term logic collapses

A temporary drawdown becomes a threat to self-worth.

Short-term noise overrides long-term strategy.

Reducing attachment restores perspective.

You begin to see losses as **part of the journey**, not judgments on your competence or value.

Practical Ways to Soften Financial Attachment

Attachment cannot be eliminated overnight.

But it can be **softened consistently**.

Practical steps include:

- Separating self-worth from net worth
- Reviewing finances at defined intervals
- Maintaining buffers that create emotional space
- Focusing on process, not daily valuation
- Accepting uncertainty as normal, not abnormal

Peace increases as the grip loosens.

The goal is not detachment from money—

but detachment from the illusion that money can remove uncertainty.

Investor Reflection – Chapter 7

Attachment: The Root of Financial Anxiety

Financial anxiety rarely comes from insufficient planning.

It comes from **emotional attachment to outcomes**.

When investors attach their sense of safety, identity, or self-worth to portfolio values, every fluctuation feels personal. Volatility becomes a threat rather than a feature.

Attachment shows up as:

- Constant portfolio checking
- Intolerance to short-term loss
- Overreaction to news
- Difficulty staying committed to long-term plans

Professionally successful investors cultivate **emotional distance**.

They care deeply about process—

but lightly about short-term outcomes.

Detachment does not mean neglect.

It means engagement without obsession.

Investors who reduce attachment:

- Make fewer impulsive decisions
- Recover faster from drawdowns
- Remain aligned with long-term goals

The calmer investor is not less serious.

They are simply **less entangled**.

Reducing attachment restores clarity—

and clarity protects capital.

Chapter Takeaway

Attachment promises security.

It delivers anxiety.

Money held too tightly creates fear.

Money held wisely creates support.

Freedom is not found in controlling outcomes—

It is found in **loosening the grip**.

Reflection Exercises – Chapter 7

1. Awareness Check

What financial outcomes am I emotionally clinging to?

2. Personal Inventory

Do I monitor money to inform decisions—or to soothe anxiety?

3. Behavior Mapping

One habit of over-monitoring I can consciously reduce.

4. Emotional Insight

Which fear arises most often—loss, uncertainty, or comparison?

5. One Quiet Commitment

One way I will practice engagement without obsession.

Chapter - 8
Mindfulness in Spending

How awareness transforms daily money habits

Why small moments of attention quietly reshape financial life

Spending Is a Mirror of the Mind

Most people believe they spend money rationally.

In reality, much of spending is **emotional, habitual, and unconscious**.

Spending decisions are often made not at the level of logic, but at the level of mood, fatigue, identity, and unexamined desire. This is why budgets frequently fail—not because they are mathematically wrong, but because they ignore the **inner state** driving behavior.

In Buddhist practice, **mindfulness (*Sati*)** is the act of noticing what is happening—clearly, gently, and without judgment. It does not suppress impulses. It observes them.

Applied to money, mindfulness does not ask only:

"Can I afford this?"

It asks something more revealing:

"What is happening inside me right now?"

That single shift—from affordability to awareness—changes spending behavior more effectively than rules, guilt, or restriction.

Unmindful spending asks:

- "Can I buy this?"

Mindful spending asks:

- "Why do I want this right now?"

One question addresses numbers.

The other addresses **causes**.

The Emotional Triggers behind Spending

Spending often follows inner states rather than actual needs.

Common patterns include:

- **Stress** inviting comfort buying
- **Fatigue** inviting convenience spending
- **Boredom** inviting browsing
- **Insecurity** inviting status spending
- **Celebration** inviting excess

These reactions are not failures of character.

They are **human responses**.

The problem is not emotion.

The problem is **automation**.

When spending becomes reflexive, awareness disappears. The mind acts before understanding arises.

Mindfulness inserts a **pause**.

And the pause restores **choice**.

Story: Rohit and the Weekend Pattern

Rohit noticed something unusual while reviewing his expense statements.

Most unplanned purchases occurred on **Friday nights and Sundays**.

After long workweeks, online shopping felt soothing. Orders were placed quickly, forgotten just as quickly—and sometimes regretted days later.

Instead of forcing discipline or cutting cards, Rohit tried something simpler: **awareness**.

For one month, he noted:

- His emotional state before spending
- The time of day
- The justification his mind offered

The pattern became unmistakable:

- Exhaustion preceded convenience spending
- Boredom preceded browsing
- Stress preceded impulse buying

Rohit introduced one gentle rule:

Delay all non-essential purchases by 24 hours.

Many impulses faded on their own.

Some purchases still happened—but without regret.

Mindfulness did not eliminate spending.

It eliminated **unconscious spending**.

And that made all the difference.

The Hidden Cost of Unmindful Spending

Unmindful spending rarely creates immediate damage.

Its cost is **gradual and cumulative**.

Over time, it leads to:

- Slow leaks in savings
- Guilt after purchases
- Dependence on consumption for emotional relief
- Erosion of financial confidence

Perhaps the most damaging cost is **loss of self-trust**.

When people repeatedly spend in ways they later regret, they begin to doubt their ability to manage money—regardless of income.

Mindful spending restores alignment between **intention and action**.

And alignment restores confidence.

Mindfulness Is Not Restriction

Mindfulness is often mistaken for denial or minimalism.

It is neither.

Mindfulness does not demand less spending.

It demands **intentional spending**.

A mindful purchase:

- Aligns with values
- Supports long-term well-being
- Fits within financial reality
- Does not create future anxiety

A mindful spender may spend generously—

and still remain peaceful.

Pleasure is not the enemy.

Unexamined repetition is.

How Awareness Changes Habits

Mindfulness does not work through perfection.

It works through **repetition**.

Each moment of awareness weakens automation.

Over time:

- Impulses lose urgency
- Emotions become signals, not commands
- Spending aligns naturally with priorities

The goal is not control.

It is **clarity**.

Practical Tools for Mindful Spending

Mindfulness becomes sustainable when supported by simple structure:

- **Pause** before purchases above a defined amount
- **Label spending** as need, comfort, joy, or status
- **Track emotions** alongside expenses for one month
- **Reduce friction for saving** (automation)
- **Increase friction for spending** (delays, limits)
- **Review monthly** without guilt or self-criticism

Awareness grows through consistency—not intensity.

Investor Reflection – Chapter 8

Mindfulness in Spending

Spending decisions often appear small, but their cumulative impact on wealth and peace is profound.

Unmindful spending is rarely about affordability.

It is about **emotion**.

Stress, boredom, celebration, and comparison quietly influence consumption. When spending becomes automatic, savings weaken—not dramatically, but persistently.

Mindful investors treat spending as a **conscious choice**, not a reflex.

They ask:

- Is this solving a real need—or a temporary feeling?
- Does this expense add lasting value—or short-term relief?

Professionally, disciplined spending:

- Preserves investable surplus
- Reduces lifestyle pressure
- Increases resilience during income fluctuations

Mindfulness does not restrict enjoyment.

It removes **regret**.

Investors who spend with awareness rarely feel deprived—

and rarely feel anxious about money.

Over time, mindful spending supports both **wealth accumulation** and **emotional stability**.

Chapter Takeaway

Money spent unconsciously leaks peace.

Money spent mindfully supports life.

The goal is not control.

It is **conscious choice**.

Reflection Exercises – Chapter 8

1. Awareness Check

What emotions most often trigger my spending?

2. Personal Inventory

Which recent purchases brought lasting value—and which did not?

3. Behavior Mapping

One spending habit I can slow down this month.

4. Emotional Insight

Do I use spending to change how I feel?

5. One Quiet Commitment

One purchase I will pause before making next time.

Chapter - 9
Greed, Fear & Delusion: The Investor's Three Poisons

How emotions distort financial decisions

Why markets rarely defeat investors—investors defeat themselves

Why Knowledge Alone Is Never Enough

If information alone created wealth, the most informed investors would never fail.

Yet history tells a different story.

Market crashes, bubbles, and repeated cycles of regret do not occur because investors lack data. They occur because **emotion overwhelms judgment**.

Financial mistakes are rarely intellectual.

They are **emotional**.

Buddhist psychology offers a precise framework for understanding this. It identifies **three mental poisons** that cloud perception and distort decision-making:

- **Greed (Lobha)**
- **Fear or Aversion (Dosa)**

- **Delusion or Ignorance (Moha)**

These poisons are dangerous precisely because they do not appear as weaknesses.

They appear as:

- Confidence
- Caution
- Conviction

That is why they quietly guide decisions—often without being noticed.

Greed: When "More" Destroys "Enough"

Greed rarely announces itself as excess.

It begins as dissatisfaction.

It whispers:

- "Just a little more."
- "Why settle for average?"
- "Everyone else is making faster money."

Greed is not always loud or reckless.

Often, it feels *reasonable.*

But greed shortens time horizons.

It makes patience feel foolish and discipline feel slow.

In investing, greed often leads to:

- Chasing recent winners
- Overconcentration in one idea

- Ignoring early risk signals
- Abandoning asset allocation
- Confusing momentum with safety

Ironically, greed most often **destroys gains already earned**, not future potential.

Story: Prakash and the Missed Exit

Prakash invested early in a fast-growing stock.

Returns were strong.

Confidence grew.

Stories multiplied.

When the price doubled, he did not rebalance—momentum felt powerful.

When it tripled, he did not reduce exposure—narratives felt convincing.

Warning signs appeared.

He noticed them—and dismissed them.

When the reversal came, it was swift.

Gains evaporated.

Shock turned into panic.

Panic turned into regret.

Later, Prakash reflected honestly:

"I didn't lose money when prices fell.

I lost it when I ignored 'enough.'"

Greed delayed action.

Discipline would have protected progress.

Fear: When Protection Becomes Paralysis

Fear is greed's mirror image.

It appears after:

- Losses
- Volatility
- Negative news
- Unexpected outcomes

Fear magnifies risk and shrinks perspective.

Fear-driven behavior includes:

- Panic selling
- Abandoning markets entirely
- Holding excessive cash
- Refusing reasonable, necessary risk

Fear feels protective.

In the short term, it reduces discomfort.

But fear has a long-term cost.

Long-term wealth is not destroyed by temporary loss.

It is destroyed by **permanent withdrawal**.

Fear prevents recovery by keeping investors absent during rebuilding phases—when patience is most rewarded.

Delusion: When Narrative Replaces Reality

Delusion is not lack of intelligence.

It is **misperception**.

In financial life, delusion appears as:

- Believing recent trends will continue indefinitely
- Mistaking luck for skill
- Following popular narratives without understanding
- Assuming complexity equals superiority

Delusion feels confident—until conditions change.

It thrives during strong trends, when evidence seems abundant and doubt feels unnecessary.

But when reality shifts, delusion collapses suddenly.

The fall is often sharper because the belief was strong.

How the Three Poisons Reinforce Each Other

These poisons rarely act alone.

They form a predictable cycle:

- **Greed** pushes entry
- **Delusion** justifies the decision
- **Fear** dictates the exit

This cycle repeats endlessly for investors without awareness.

Each round weakens confidence, discipline, and trust in process.

Breaking the cycle does not require superior prediction.

It requires **mindful distance**.

Antidotes to the Three Poisons

Buddhist wisdom does not suppress emotion.

It **balances** it.

Each poison has a practical antidote:

- **Against Greed → Discipline**
  - Predefined rules
  - Rebalancing
  - Sufficient-return mindset
- **Against Fear → Perspective**
  - Long-term horizon
  - Diversification
  - Historical context
- **Against Delusion → Humility**
  - Continuous learning
  - Simplicity over complexity
  - Respect for uncertainty

Awareness allows emotion to arise—without allowing it to decide.

The Investor's Real Edge

Markets test intelligence.

They expose temperament.

The greatest edge in investing is not:

- Speed
- Access to information
- Superior forecasts

It is **emotional mastery**.

Investors who survive and compound over decades are not those who avoid emotion—but those who **recognize it early** and refuse to act from it.

Investor Reflection – Chapter 9

Greed, Fear & Delusion — The Investor's Three Poisons

Investment mistakes rarely arise from lack of information.

They arise from emotions overpowering judgment.

Greed pushes investors to chase performance beyond logic.

Fear pushes them to abandon sound plans during discomfort.

Delusion convinces them that trends, narratives, or recent success will continue indefinitely.

These three often work together:

- Greed encourages entry
- Delusion justifies it
- Fear dictates exit

Professionally successful investors recognize these emotions early—not to suppress them, but to prevent them from deciding.

They rely on:

- Predefined asset allocation
- Diversification
- Disciplined rebalancing
- Long-term perspective

Markets reward those who manage emotion better than information.

The true edge is not prediction.

It is **awareness under pressure**.

Chapter Takeaway

Greed, fear, and delusion are natural.

Letting them decide is optional.

Investors who master emotion quietly outperform those who chase information.

Reflection Exercises – Chapter 9

1. Awareness Check

Which emotion dominates my financial decisions most often—greed, fear, or overconfidence?

2. Personal Inventory

When did emotion last override my plan?

3. Behavior Mapping

One rule that would protect me from impulsive action.

4. Emotional Insight

Do gains make me reckless—or losses make me rigid?

5. One Quiet Commitment

One emotional habit I will observe before acting next time.

PART - IV
Wealth, Simplicity & Inner Freedom

EMI

Chapter - 10
Contentment (Santutthi): The Highest Wealth

Why "enough" is a powerful financial strategy

How inner sufficiency protects outer prosperity

Why More So Often Fails to Satisfy

Modern life teaches a simple equation:

More equals better.

More income.

More comfort.

More experiences.

More recognition.

Yet dissatisfaction persists—even among those who achieve what they once desired.

This contradiction lies at the heart of modern financial anxiety.

Buddhist philosophy offers a counterintuitive but deeply practical insight:

Contentment is not the reward of wealth; it is the condition for peace.

Contentment (*Santutthi*) does not reject growth, progress, or ambition.

It rejects **dependence on growth for emotional stability**.

When contentment is absent:

- No income feels sufficient
- Milestones lose meaning quickly
- Satisfaction is postponed to the future

When contentment is present:

- Even modest wealth feels adequate
- Progress is appreciated
- Life is not placed on hold

Contentment changes not *what* you pursue, but *how* you relate to pursuit.

Contentment vs. Complacency

Contentment is often misunderstood as settling, slowing down, or lowering standards.

This is a serious misunderstanding.

The difference is subtle—but crucial.

- **Complacency** avoids effort, responsibility, and growth
- **Contentment** removes anxiety while effort continues

A contented person may strive intensely—but without inner pressure.

Ambition becomes purposeful rather than compulsive.

In financial life, contentment:

- Reduces comparison
- Stabilizes decision-making
- Protects against reckless expansion
- Enhances gratitude and perspective

It allows progress **without restlessness**.

Story: Suresh and the Quiet Shift

Suresh spent years chasing financial milestones.

Each achievement brought relief—

followed quickly by a new target.

Salary increases, investments, and recognition all arrived.

Yet satisfaction never stayed.

After reaching what he once considered *"enough,"* he noticed something unsettling: the feeling of arrival lasted only weeks.

During a casual family conversation, his father said:

"We worked hard so you wouldn't worry like we did.

If you still worry, something else needs attention."

That sentence stayed with him.

Suresh began to question assumptions he had never examined.

He quietly redefined success:

- Stability over constant upgrades
- Meaningful work over endless scaling
- Time, health, and relationships as assets

Nothing dramatic changed externally.

Internally, pressure eased.

Contentment did not reduce his income.

It reduced his **restlessness**.

Why Contentment Is Financially Powerful

Contentment is not passive.

It is **strategic**.

A contented person:

- Saves naturally
- Avoids impulsive upgrades
- Invests patiently
- Gives without fear
- Tolerates delayed gratification

They are less vulnerable to:

- Advertising pressure
- Social comparison
- Fear of missing out

- Performance envy

During market cycles, contentment acts as an emotional shock absorber:

- Reducing panic in downturns
- Reducing excess in upturns

Where others react, the contented investor remains steady.

The Illusion of the Finish Line

Desire promises arrival.

Contentment recognizes presence.

Without contentment:

- Milestones feel temporary
- Satisfaction depends on future gains
- Joy is postponed

With contentment:

- Milestones are appreciated
- Growth is enjoyed without urgency
- Life is lived alongside ambition

Contentment does not stop progress.

It stops **chronic dissatisfaction**.

It allows joy **now**, not after the next achievement.

Cultivating Contentment in Financial Life

Contentment is not inherited.

It is **practiced**.

Practical ways to cultivate it include:

- Clearly defining your personal version of *"enough"*
- Practicing gratitude for financial stability already achieved
- Reducing exposure to constant comparison (social, professional, digital)
- Measuring progress annually—not socially
- Separating joy, identity, and self-worth from consumption

Contentment grows through **awareness**, not denial.

Investor Reflection – Chapter 10

Contentment (Santutthi): The Highest Wealth

Many investors believe dissatisfaction is necessary for progress.

In reality, **chronic dissatisfaction leads to poor decisions**.

Contentment does not eliminate ambition.

It removes **restlessness**.

Investors without contentment often:

- Keep shifting goals
- Increase risk unnecessarily
- Feel constant pressure to outperform

- Struggle to enjoy progress

Contented investors:

- Define *"enough"* clearly
- Invest with patience
- Resist comparison-driven decisions
- Remain calm during volatility

Professionally, contentment acts as an emotional stabilizer.

It reduces the urge to chase returns beyond what goals require.

When investors know what is sufficient, they stop exposing themselves to avoidable risk.

Contentment protects wealth—not by limiting growth,

But by **preventing self-sabotage**.

Chapter Takeaway

Contentment is invisible wealth.

It protects visible wealth.

Those who master *"enough"* rarely feel poor—

Regardless of numbers.

Reflection Exercises – Chapter 10

1. Awareness Check

When do I feel most dissatisfied—despite being financially secure?

2. Personal Inventory

What does *"enough"* mean for me today—not someday?

3. Behavior Mapping

One comparison I can consciously step back from this month.

4. Emotional Insight

Do my financial goals arise from purpose—or pressure?

5. One Quiet Commitment

One way I will practice contentment without reducing effort.

Chapter - 11
Saving as Self-Compassion

Why planning is an act of care, not fear

How preparedness reduces anxiety and restores dignity

Reframing Saving: From Restriction to Care

Saving is often misunderstood as denial—

As something done *instead of* living well.

In many households, saving carries a quiet emotional burden. It is associated with restraint, sacrifice, or missing out. Spending feels alive. Saving feels defensive.

Buddhist wisdom offers a gentler and far more accurate frame:

Saving is compassion directed toward your future self.

Compassion anticipates suffering and reduces it where possible.

Saving does the same.

It acknowledges uncertainty without panic.

It prepares without obsession.

Saving quietly says:

- "I accept that change is natural."
- "I respect my future needs."
- "I choose steadiness over anxiety."

This is not fear.This is **care**.

Why Many People Resist Saving

Resistance to saving rarely comes from income alone.

It comes from **beliefs and emotional narratives**.

Common inner voices include:

- "I'll start once I earn more."
- "Saving means I'm missing out on life."
- "Planning feels pessimistic."
- "The future will work itself out."

These beliefs confuse optimism with avoidance.

Uncertainty is not pessimism.

It is **reality**.

Saving does not prepare for catastrophe.

It prepares for **change**—which is inevitable.

Avoiding saving does not eliminate uncertainty.

It only delays meeting it.

Story: Anjali and the Sudden Pause

Anjali lived comfortably.

Her expenses were reasonable.

Her income was steady.

Savings existed—but irregularly.

Life felt stable—until it wasn't.

A sudden organizational restructuring ended her role. Income stopped. Decisions became urgent. Anxiety filled the silence that followed routine.

The shock was not unemployment.

It was **vulnerability**.

She realized she had options—but very little time.

After stability returned, Anjali did not become anxious or restrictive. She changed one habit:

She **saved first**.

She built an emergency fund slowly, without pressure or guilt. No dramatic lifestyle changes. No self-punishment. Just quiet consistency.

Months later, something unexpected happened.

Life felt calmer.

Not because risks vanished—

But because **resilience appeared**.

Anjali reflected:

"Saving didn't increase my income.

It increased my sense of safety."

Saving Reduces Cognitive Load

Money stress is not only financial.

It is **mental**.

When savings are absent:

- Every expense feels urgent
- Every risk feels threatening
- Every decision feels heavy

Without buffers, the mind remains on alert.

When savings exist:

- Decisions feel calmer
- Risks are assessed more rationally
- Patience increases
- Panic reduces

Saving buys **time**.

Time buys **clarity**.

And clarity improves every financial decision that follows.

The Middle Path: Saving Without Hoarding

Buddhism consistently warns against extremes.

Saving is no exception.

- **No saving** creates vulnerability.
- **Excessive saving** creates rigidity, fear, and emotional contraction.

Healthy saving lies in balance—

adequate buffers without obsession.

Saving becomes unhealthy when it is driven by:

- Anxiety
- Distrust of life
- Inability to enjoy the present

Saving remains healthy when it is driven by:

- Care
- Preparation
- Self-respect

The intention matters more than the amount.

Practical Saving Wisdom

Saving works best when it is **quiet and consistent**, not dramatic.

Simple, effective principles include:

- Save before spending, not after
- Build emergency funds before aggressive investing
- Automate savings to reduce emotional friction
- Increase saving gradually as income grows
- Review annually—not obsessively

Saving should not dominate attention.

It should **remove itself from attention** by being reliable.

Saving as Self-Respect

Saving is a form of **delayed self-respect**.

It quietly affirms:

- "My future matters."
- "I deserve stability."
- "I choose preparation over regret."

This mindset transforms saving from sacrifice into dignity.

You are not withholding from yourself.

You are **standing with yourself—across time**.

Investor Reflection – Chapter 11

Saving as Self-Compassion

Saving is often framed as sacrifice.

In reality, it is care for one's future self.

Investors who lack adequate savings live under constant pressure. Every market movement feels urgent. Every decision feels high-stakes. This emotional strain often leads to reactive behavior and poor timing.

Savings create **psychological space**.

Professionally, adequate buffers:

- Reduce panic during volatility
- Allow patience in investing
- Prevent forced liquidation
- Improve decision quality

Investors who save consistently are not pessimistic.

They are **realistic**.

Saving does not mean preparing for disaster.

It means preparing for change.

When emergency funds exist, investors tolerate uncertainty better. They stay invested longer. They think clearly under pressure.

Saving with compassion transforms money from a source of fear into a source of **stability**.

Chapter Takeaway

Saving is not about mistrusting life.

It is about **trusting yourself** to handle life.

Money saved with compassion becomes emotional strength.

Reflection Exercises – Chapter 11

1. Awareness Check

Do I view saving as restriction—or protection?

2. Personal Inventory

How would my decisions change with a stronger financial buffer?

3. Behavior Mapping

One step I can take to make saving automatic and effortless.

4. Emotional Insight

Does my saving behavior come from fear—or care?

5. One Quiet Commitment

One way I will treat my future self with more compassion.

Chapter - 12
Debt: Modern Bondage

How borrowing quietly steals future freedom

Why the real cost of debt is not interest, but loss of choice

When Tomorrow Is Spent Today

Debt offers a simple promise: relief now, payment later.

Used consciously, borrowing can support growth—education, shelter, or productive capacity. Used unconsciously, it becomes a form of **modern bondage**.

In Buddhist thought, suffering arises when **desire overrides awareness**. Debt is desire given a repayment schedule. It feels light at the beginning and heavy over time.

Debt rarely announces danger.

It arrives as convenience.

It settles in as normal.

And only later does it reveal its weight.

The danger of debt lies not in borrowing itself, but in **forgetting the future** while satisfying the present.

Why Debt Feels Manageable—Until It Isn't

Modern systems are designed to make borrowing feel painless.

- EMIs that appear small and manageable
- Buy-now-pay-later schemes that delay discomfort
- Credit structures that hide total future cost

At the start, debt feels controlled.

Over time, control quietly reverses.

As fixed obligations accumulate:

- Flexibility disappears
- Risk tolerance collapses
- Opportunities feel threatening
- Anxiety becomes background noise

The cost of debt is not only interest.

It is **lost agency**.

When future income is already assigned, freedom shrinks—regardless of how high income appears.

Story: Vikram and the Shrinking Horizon

Vikram earned well and lived comfortably.

His lifestyle was funded by predictable EMIs—home, car, gadgets, travel. Everything was affordable. Nothing felt reckless.

Yet Vikram felt trapped.

Job dissatisfaction lingered, but change felt impossible. New opportunities appeared risky. Every month began with commitments already decided.

One evening, Vikram calculated something he had never looked at honestly:

How many future months of income were already promised?

The number unsettled him.

Debt had not ruined him.

It had **narrowed his horizon**.

As Vikram began reducing debt deliberately—not dramatically—relief arrived before freedom. Choices returned gradually. Confidence followed.

Nothing about his income changed immediately.

His **sense of possibility** did.

The Psychological Cost of Debt

Debt quietly trains the mind.

Over time, it conditions people to:

- Prioritize certainty over growth
- Avoid healthy risk
- Accept pressure as normal
- Equate income with survival

This mental conditioning reduces resilience.

People with heavy debt often:

- Tolerate unsatisfying work longer
- Fear income disruption excessively
- Panic sooner during volatility
- Make conservative decisions out of necessity, not strategy

Debt-free living is not austerity.

It is **optionality**.

The Buddhist View: Borrowing without Craving

Buddhism does not forbid borrowing.

It warns against **craving-driven borrowing**.

Wise borrowing:

- Supports productivity or shelter
- Has clear repayment capacity
- Preserves dignity and flexibility

Unwise borrowing:

- Funds desire, comparison, or convenience
- Expands lifestyle without buffers
- Creates psychological captivity

The same loan can be freedom or bondage—

Depending on **intention, capacity, and awareness**.

Debt taken with clarity remains light.

Debt taken with craving becomes heavy.

From Obligation to Choice

Freedom is not the absence of responsibility.

It is the **presence of choice**.

Reducing debt:

- Increases calm
- Restores patience
- Expands opportunity
- Strengthens self-trust

Even partial debt reduction brings relief.

Because each obligation removed returns **time, energy, and attention**.

Debt reduction rarely feels exciting.

But its emotional impact is immediate.

Why Debt Reduces Investment Intelligence

High fixed obligations change how people invest.

When debt is heavy:

- Volatility feels threatening
- Long-term investing feels risky
- Liquidity becomes obsession
- Panic decisions become likely

Debt does not just consume cash flow.

It consumes **emotional bandwidth**.

Investors with low or well-managed debt think differently. They act from strategy, not pressure. They tolerate uncertainty without panic.

Practical Wisdom on Debt

Debt clarity is more important than debt avoidance.

Practical principles include:

- Avoid debt for pure consumption
- Prioritize high-interest debt reduction
- Understand total future obligation—not just emi
- Preserve emergency buffers even while reducing debt
- Choose freedom over lifestyle inflation

Debt freedom compounds faster than income growth—

because freedom improves every decision that follows.

Investor Reflection – Chapter 12

Debt: Modern Bondage

Debt rarely feels dangerous at the beginning.

It feels manageable, justified, and even empowering.

Over time, however, debt quietly reduces **financial flexibility**—the most underappreciated asset in investing.

Investors burdened with high fixed obligations:

- Lose risk tolerance
- Panic sooner during volatility

- Avoid long-term opportunities
- Prioritize certainty over growth

Debt does not only consume cash flow.

It consumes **choice**.

Professionally, investors with low or well-managed debt:

- Think long-term
- Invest patiently
- Withstand income disruptions
- Act from strategy, not pressure

Borrowing for productivity or shelter can be constructive.

Borrowing for consumption, comparison, or convenience often becomes psychological captivity.

Reducing debt restores calm **before** it increases wealth.

Freedom compounds faster than leverage.

Chapter Takeaway

Debt does not enslave instantly.

It trains obedience slowly.

Reducing debt restores peace long before wealth increases.

Reflection Exercises – Chapter 12

1. Awareness Check

How much of my future income is already committed?

2. Personal Inventory

Which debts genuinely improve my life—and which restrict it?

3. Behavior Mapping

One step I can take to reduce dependency on borrowing.

4. Emotional Insight

What emotion drives my borrowing—desire, fear, or comparison?

5. One Quiet Commitment

One choice I will make that prioritizes flexibility over convenience.

PART - V
Investing with Wisdom

Chapter - 13
Patience (Khanti) & Long-Term Investing

Why time, not intelligence, builds wealth

How staying power quietly outperforms brilliance

The Most Underrated Financial Skill

In a world that celebrates speed, patience feels almost revolutionary.

Instant results, real-time updates, constant notifications, and endless comparison train us to expect quick validation. Progress is measured in days, sometimes minutes. Anything slow is dismissed as ineffective.

Buddhist philosophy offers a radically different insight. It identifies **Khanti—patience**—not as weakness, but as a **quiet strength** that sustains effort when outcomes remain invisible.

Patience is often misunderstood.

It is not:

- Waiting passively
- Avoiding decisions

- Tolerating injustice or inertia

Patience is something far more demanding.

Patience is continuing with discipline while results remain unseen.

In investing, this distinction is crucial.

Why Impatience Is So Expensive

Impatience does not usually appear as recklessness.

It often appears as **reasonable action**.

- Switching strategies too soon
- Abandoning plans during temporary discomfort
- Chasing recent performers
- Reacting to short-term volatility
- "optimizing" portfolios too frequently

Each action feels small.

Each feels justified.

Together, they interrupt one powerful force: **compounding**.

Markets reward consistency.

They punish restlessness.

Impatience is expensive not because it fails immediately—but because it **resets progress repeatedly**.

Story: Deepak and the Early Exit

Deepak invested systematically for several years.

Returns were not spectacular, but they were steady. His plan was sound. His goals were realistic.

Then came a market correction.

Portfolio values declined. Headlines turned negative. Conversations grew fearful. Doubt replaced quiet confidence.

Believing he could "wait for clarity," Deepak exited his investments.

The decision felt cautious.

It felt intelligent.

Months later, markets recovered. Prices moved higher. Confidence returned.

Deepak re-entered—at higher levels.

The loss was not dramatic.

But it was **avoidable**.

Later, he reflected honestly:

"I didn't lose money because markets fell.

I lost it because I couldn't stay."

Patience would not have prevented volatility.

It would have allowed **time to do its work**.

Compounding Rewards Those Who Stay

Compounding is often celebrated—but rarely respected.

It does not impress early.

It does not reward activity.

It requires **uninterrupted time**.

The greatest gains in investing occur not because of exceptional intelligence, but because of **duration**.

Every unnecessary exit breaks compounding.

Every emotional interruption delays it.

Time rewards discipline, not urgency.

This is why many intelligent investors underperform simpler strategies. They interfere too often with processes that already work.

Patience as Emotional Strength

Patience is not merely a financial skill.

It is an **emotional capacity**.

Patience tolerates:

- Boredom during slow growth
- Discomfort during volatility
- Uncertainty without panic
- Long periods without validation

This is not blind optimism.

It is **trust in process**.

Patience allows investors to remain steady while others react emotionally—selling in fear, buying in excitement, and exhausting themselves in between.

The Buddhist Insight Applied to Markets

Buddhism teaches endurance **without attachment**.

Applied to investing, patience means:

- Committing to long-term plans
- Accepting temporary discomfort
- Resisting the urge for constant action
- Allowing outcomes to unfold

Activity feels productive.

Stillness often is.

Markets do not reward constant action.

They reward **appropriate action—and long pauses**.

Why Doing Nothing Is Often the Hardest Work

In investing, the most difficult action is often **inaction**.

Not because it is easy—but because it requires:

- Confidence without applause
- Discipline without excitement
- Faith without certainty

Most wealth is created in **uneventful years**, not dramatic ones.

Patience allows investors to benefit from those years quietly.

Practical Applications of Patience

Patience becomes effective when supported by structure.

Practical ways to cultivate it include:

- Defining clear investment horizons
- Using systematic investing methods
- Avoiding frequent portfolio monitoring
- Rebalancing periodically, not reactively
- Judging decisions by process, not short-term outcome

Patience simplifies complexity by removing unnecessary decisions.

Investor Reflection – Chapter 13

Patience (Khanti) & Long-Term Investing

In investing, patience is not passive waiting.

It is **active consistency**.

Most investors understand compounding intellectually—but interrupt it emotionally. They change strategies too soon, exit during discomfort, or chase short-term performance, resetting progress again and again.

Patience protects compounding by **preventing unnecessary interference**.

Professionally disciplined investors:

- Stay invested through uneventful years
- Allow time to do heavy lifting

- Resist the urge to "improve" what already works
- Judge decisions over full cycles, not short phases

Impatience is expensive because it feels reasonable.

Patience feels boring—but it is profitable.

Markets reward those who can tolerate:

- Slow progress
- Temporary underperformance
- Long periods without validation

The real advantage is not intelligence or timing.

It is the ability to **stay**.

Chapter Takeaway

Patience is not passive waiting.

It is **active staying**.

Those who stay long enough rarely regret it.

Reflection Exercises – Chapter 13

1. Awareness Check

In which areas of my financial life do I feel most impatient?

2. Personal Inventory

When did impatience last cause me to change plans prematurely?

3. Behavior Mapping

One habit I can adopt to reduce unnecessary action.

4. Emotional Insight

Does discomfort make me act—or make me observe?

5. One Quiet Commitment

One decision I will allow time to work on before intervening.

Chapter - 14
Silence, Boredom & Long-Term Wealth

Why most wealth is created when nothing seems to be happening

How stillness quietly outperforms excitement

The Unspoken Enemy of Long-Term Investors

Fear gets attention.

Greed gets headlines.

But **boredom** quietly destroys more wealth than both.

Most investors do not fail because they panic at the bottom or chase the top. They fail because they cannot remain steady when nothing dramatic is happening.

Markets often spend long periods in silence:

- Returns are moderate
- Headlines are dull
- Portfolios move slowly
- Progress feels invisible

This is precisely when discipline erodes.

Boredom does not feel dangerous.

It feels *reasonable*.

And that is why it is so costly.

Why Boredom Feels like Something Is "Wrong"

Human psychology is wired for stimulation.

Action feels productive.

Silence feels suspicious.

When markets are uneventful, the mind begins to question:

- "Am I doing enough?"
- "Should I change something?"
- "Others seem to be making faster money."
- "Is my strategy outdated?"

Nothing is actually broken.

But boredom creates the **illusion of inefficiency**.

This illusion leads to:

- Unnecessary portfolio churn
- Frequent fund switching
- Abandoning sips prematurely
- Chasing excitement disguised as opportunity

In reality, boredom is often a sign that the system is **working exactly as intended**.

Why SIP Discipline Dies in Quiet Years

Systematic investing does not succeed because of spectacular rallies.

It succeeds because of **ordinary consistency**.

Yet most SIP discontinuations happen not during crashes—but during quiet years, when:

- Returns are average
- Markets move sideways
- Patience is tested
- Enthusiasm fades

Boredom whispers:

"Pause it for now."

"Let's wait for clarity."

"I'll restart later."

Later rarely comes.

Compounding does not collapse loudly.

It dissolves **quietly**—through interruption.

What appears to be a small pause becomes a permanent leak in long-term wealth.

"Doing Nothing" Feels Irresponsible — But Often Isn't

Modern culture equates responsibility with activity.

We are conditioned to believe:

- Action equals intelligence

- Movement equals control
- Stillness equals negligence

This belief spills into financial life.

Investors feel compelled to:

- Constantly review
- Adjust strategies
- React to information
- Justify activity

But markets do not reward constant action.

They reward **appropriate inactivity**.

Not laziness.

Not neglect.

But **intentional stillness**.

Knowing when *not* to act is as important as knowing when to act.

Buddhist Stillness vs. Modern Overactivity

Buddhist philosophy treats stillness as strength.

Silence is not emptiness.

It is **clarity without noise**.

In meditation, nothing appears to happen—yet transformation occurs.

Financial stillness works the same way.

During uneventful periods:

- Discipline deepens
- Emotional reactivity weakens
- Habits solidify
- Compounding quietly accelerates

Modern overactivity confuses stimulation with progress.

Buddhist stillness understands a deeper truth:

Progress is often invisible while it is happening.

The Hidden Power of Uneventful Years

Most meaningful wealth is created in years no one remembers.

Not during:

- Crashes
- Bubbles
- Dramatic recoveries

But during long stretches of:

- Moderate returns
- Regular investing
- Quiet discipline

These years feel forgettable.

They are **foundational**.

The investor who survives boredom intact often outperforms the one who survives fear heroically.

Story: The Investor Who Almost "Optimized" Away His Wealth

Rajesh had a solid plan.

Diversified investments.

Regular SIPs.

Clear long-term goals.

For years, nothing dramatic happened.

Returns were steady—but unspectacular.

Friends discussed faster gains elsewhere.

Online commentary suggested smarter, more active strategies.

Rajesh began to feel uneasy.

Not fearful—**restless**.

He considered:

- Switching funds
- Timing entries
- Trying something "more active"

Before acting, he paused.

He realized something crucial:

Nothing in my plan is broken.

Only my tolerance for boredom is.

He changed nothing.

Years later, Rajesh noticed something quietly powerful:

His wealth had grown substantially—

without stress,

without drama,

without constant decision-making.

Boredom had been the price of peace—and **compounding**.

Why Boredom Is a Sign of Maturity

Early investing feels exciting.

Later investing feels quiet.

That transition is not loss of opportunity.

It is **progress**.

Boredom indicates:

- Systems are in place
- Emotions are stabilizing
- Impulse is losing authority
- Long-term thinking is taking root

This is where serious wealth is built.

Not through brilliance.

Through **endurance**.

How to Protect Yourself from Boredom-Induced Mistakes

Boredom cannot be eliminated—but it can be managed.

Practical anchors include:

- Defining long review intervals
- Automating investments

- Reducing financial noise intake
- Measuring progress annually, not weekly
- Accepting that uneventful periods are necessary

A simple reminder helps:

If nothing is demanding action,

action is probably not required.

Investor Reflection – Chapter 14

Silence, Boredom & Long-Term Wealth

Most long-term wealth is not created by making brilliant decisions.

It is created by **avoiding unnecessary ones**.

Boredom tempts investors to interfere with well-functioning plans. Sideways markets and moderate returns create the illusion that something must be changed—even when nothing is broken.

Professionally mature investors respect quiet periods.

They understand that:

- Markets do not need constant supervision
- Portfolios do not require frequent adjustment
- Discipline outperforms excitement

Boredom is not a signal of failure.

It is often a sign that systems are working.

Investors who tolerate boredom:

- Maintain SIP discipline
- Avoid excessive churn
- Allow compounding to work uninterrupted

Quiet consistency is not inactivity.

It is **mastery over impulse**.

Chapter Takeaway

Fear tests courage.

Greed tests restraint.

Boredom tests commitment.

Those who pass boredom quietly

Often arrive where others only speak about.

Stillness is not stagnation.

It is long-term wealth in motion—**unseen**.

Reflection Exercises – Chapter 14

1. Where do I feel most restless in my financial life?
2. Do I confuse activity with progress?
3. Which systems are working quietly that I'm tempted to disturb?
4. Can I tolerate uneventful periods without interference?
5. One commitment to remain still when nothing is broken.

Chapter - 15
Non-Attachment to Outcomes

Why process matters more than prediction

How releasing control restores clarity, discipline, and calm

The Hidden Source of Financial Anxiety

Most financial anxiety is not caused by loss.

It is caused by **expectation**.

We expect markets to reward effort immediately.

We expect plans to deliver predictable results.

We expect control in a world defined by uncertainty.

When reality fails to meet these expectations, anxiety appears—not because something is broken, but because expectations were unrealistic.

Buddhist philosophy offers a liberating distinction:

We control effort and intention, not outcomes.

Non-attachment to outcomes does not mean disengagement, indifference, or carelessness.

It means **commitment without obsession**.

You act responsibly, prepare thoughtfully, and then release the demand that reality must cooperate on your timeline.

This distinction quietly dissolves much of the stress associated with money.

Why Outcome Obsession Distorts Decisions

When outcomes dominate attention, behavior changes subtly—but decisively.

Outcome obsession causes:

- Short-term volatility to feel threatening
- Prediction to replace preparation
- Emotions to override process
- Peace to become conditional on results

Investing then turns into emotional labor.

Every market movement feels personal.

Every temporary underperformance feels like failure.

Every decision is judged immediately—often unfairly.

Process-focused individuals think differently.

They measure success by:

- Consistency
- Discipline
- Alignment with long-term goals
- Quality of decision-making

They accept variability **without surrendering stability**.

This shift—from outcome to process—is one of the most important psychological upgrades an investor can make.

Story: Arjun and the Prediction Trap

Arjun was deeply engaged with markets.

He followed forecasts relentlessly.

He consumed opinions daily.

He tracked experts across platforms.

Agreement felt reassuring.

Disagreement felt unsettling.

Despite his effort, results remained inconsistent. Confidence fluctuated with every new forecast.

Over time, fatigue set in.

Arjun simplified.

He reduced information intake.

He defined a clear asset allocation.

He created predefined rebalancing rules.

He stopped trying to be *right* about the future.

Stress reduced almost immediately.

Returns improved gradually.

Arjun realized something fundamental:

> *"I was attached to being right, not to doing right."*

Non-attachment restored clarity.

The market did not change.

His relationship with it did.

Process Is the Only Reliable Control

In financial life, control is limited—but powerful when respected.

You control:

- How much you save
- How consistently you invest
- How diversified your portfolio is
- How you respond to volatility

You do not control:

- Market cycles
- Global events
- Interest rate decisions
- Short-term returns

Anxiety often arises from focusing energy where control does not exist.

Freedom comes from placing effort where it **does**.

Process becomes the anchor.

Outcomes become information—not judgment.

Non-Attachment Refines Effort

Non-attachment does not weaken discipline.

It **purifies** it.

When attachment to outcomes dissolves:

- Overtrading reduces
- Panic reactions soften
- Ego-driven decisions lose urgency

And what replaces them is subtle but powerful:

- Patience
- Resilience
- Long-term alignment
- Emotional steadiness

You still act carefully.

You simply stop demanding guarantees.

This creates a calm, professional posture—one that withstands uncertainty without becoming rigid.

Why Good Decisions Can Feel Uncomfortable

One of the hardest truths in investing is this:

- Good decisions can have bad short-term outcomes
- Bad decisions can appear successful for a while

Outcome-attached investors misread these signals.

They abandon good processes too early and reinforce poor ones because they *seem* to work.

Non-attachment allows investors to tolerate this ambiguity.

They judge decisions over **full cycles**, not short phases.

This is how discipline survives volatility.

Prediction vs Preparation

Prediction promises certainty.

Preparation builds resilience.

Prediction asks:

- "What will happen next?"

Preparation asks:

- "How will I behave regardless?"

Markets punish prediction.

They reward preparation.

Non-attachment shifts energy away from forecasting and toward structure—where it actually matters.

Practical Tools to Practice Non-Attachment

Non-attachment becomes sustainable when supported by systems.

Practical anchors include:

- Defining rules **before** emotions arise
- Reviewing performance periodically—not constantly
- Accepting volatility as normal, not exceptional
- Judging decisions by logic and process, not outcome
- Documenting reasoning at the time of decision

Let **process** be the anchor.

Let outcomes be feedback—not verdict.

Investor Reflection – Chapter 15

Non-Attachment to Outcomes

Outcome obsession is one of the most common sources of investor stress.

When investors demand certainty from an uncertain system, every fluctuation feels personal. Short-term underperformance is interpreted as failure—even when the long-term process remains sound.

Professionally successful investors shift focus from outcomes to **behavioral consistency**.

They understand:

- Effort does not guarantee immediate reward
- Discipline does not eliminate volatility
- Results are noisy in the short term

Non-attachment allows investors to:

- Remain disciplined during uncertainty
- Avoid emotional exits
- Evaluate decisions rationally over time

This does not mean ignoring results.

It means refusing to let results **dominate judgment**.

Markets reward those who commit to process and release the need to be right all the time.

Stability of mind often becomes the **greatest competitive advantage**.

Chapter Takeaway

Outcomes fluctuate.

Process endures.

Those who release obsession with results gain something more valuable than certainty—

Stability of mind.

Reflection Exercises – Chapter 15

1. **Awareness Check**

Where in my financial life am I demanding certainty?

2. **Personal Inventory**

How often do I judge decisions solely by short-term results?

3. **Behavior Mapping**

One rule or process I can strengthen to reduce emotional reactions.

4. **Emotional Insight**

Do I seek prediction to feel safe—or preparation to be steady?

5. **One Quiet Commitment**

One way I will prioritize process over outcome this month.

Chapter - 16
Right Intention in Wealth Creation

Why your "why" matters more than your "how"

How clarity of purpose shapes risk, satisfaction, and legacy

When Wealth Grows Without Direction

Money is not neutral in its effect.

It amplifies what already exists.

When intention is unclear, wealth magnifies confusion.

When intention is clear, wealth becomes a precise and powerful tool.

In Buddhist philosophy, **Right Intention (*Sammā Saṅkappa*)** refers to the motivations that guide action. It does not ask *what* you do, but *why* you do it.

In financial life, intention quietly shapes:

- Risk tolerance
- Time horizon
- Ethical boundaries
- Satisfaction with outcomes

- Emotional response to success and failure

Two people can earn the same income, build similar portfolios, and yet live entirely different inner lives—because their intentions differ.

Wealth does not create peace or pressure by itself.

Intention decides which one grows.

Why Intention Outlasts Strategy

Strategies evolve.

Intentions endure.

Markets change.

Careers shift.

Opportunities appear and disappear.

A clear intention provides **continuity** when circumstances fluctuate.

When intention is driven by fear or comparison:

- Urgency increases
- Shortcuts feel tempting
- Ethics feel negotiable
- Satisfaction feels temporary

When intention is guided by stability, growth, and contribution:

- Patience becomes natural
- Ethics feel non-negotiable
- Ambition becomes grounded

- Success feels settled

Right intention acts as a **compass**, not a constraint.

It does not limit options.

It prevents drift.

Story: Nitin and the Empty Target

Nitin achieved financial goals early.

Income was strong.

Assets grew steadily.

From the outside, he had *"made it."*

Inside, something felt incomplete.

Each milestone brought brief relief—followed by familiar restlessness. There was always another target: larger, faster, higher.

During a reflective conversation, a mentor asked him a simple question:

"If your income stopped growing today, what would still matter?"

Nitin struggled to answer.

That pause changed his approach.

He began aligning wealth with meaning:

- Choosing projects aligned with his values
- Allocating time and money to causes he cared about
- Defining a stable sense of *"enough"*

Income remained healthy.

Anxiety reduced.

Nitin learned a quiet truth:

Achievement creates numbers.

Intention creates satisfaction.

Right Intention Simplifies Financial Decisions

When intention is unclear, every decision feels heavy.

You ask:

- "Is this the best possible return?"
- "What will others think?"
- "Am I falling behind?"

When intention is clear, decisions simplify.

You stop asking:

- "Will this make me look successful?"

You start asking:

- "Does this support the life I want to live?"

Right intention filters choices during:

- Market volatility
- Career transitions
- Financial temptation
- Sudden opportunity

It becomes an inner reference point when external signals conflict.

From Identity to Responsibility

One of the most subtle shifts in wealth creation is this:

When wealth becomes **identity**, loss threatens self-worth.

When wealth becomes **responsibility**, it demands wisdom.

Right intention reframes money:

- From ego reinforcement to life support
- From comparison to contribution
- From accumulation to stewardship

This shift reduces pressure and increases purpose.

Money no longer has to prove anything.

It simply has to **serve well**.

Why Intention Shapes Risk

Risk tolerance is not only financial.

It is **psychological**.

Investors driven by fear:

- Oscillate between caution and aggression
- Overreact to volatility
- Struggle with consistency

Investors driven by ego:

- Take risk to prove competence
- Chase visibility

- Confuse boldness with wisdom

Investors guided by right intention:

- Take risk consciously, not compulsively
- Accept volatility without panic
- Align risk with purpose, not emotion

Intention determines not just *how much* risk you take—but **why you can tolerate it**.

Practical Ways to Clarify Intention

Right intention does not emerge automatically.

It is **examined and refined**.

Ask—and write—the answers to:

- Why do I want wealth?
- What problem does money truly solve for me?
- At what point does more stop adding meaning?
- How do I want my wealth to affect others?

Revisit these answers annually.

Intention evolves—but clarity protects against drift.

Investor Reflection – Chapter 16

Right Intention in Wealth Creation

Most investors focus intensely on **how** to create wealth.

Very few pause to examine **why** they want it.

Yet intention quietly shapes every financial decision.

When intention is unclear, wealth amplifies confusion:

- Risk appetite fluctuates
- Goals keep shifting
- Satisfaction remains temporary
- Comparison never ends

When intention is clear, decision-making simplifies.

Professionally grounded investors understand a core truth:

Money magnifies motive.

If the motive is fear, wealth increases anxiety.

If the motive is ego, wealth increases restlessness.

If the motive is stability, dignity, and contribution, wealth increases calm.

Right intention does not limit ambition.

It **directs** ambition.

Investors with clear intention:

- Take risk consciously, not compulsively
- Stop chasing returns beyond what goals require
- Resist pressure to "prove" success
- Measure progress by alignment, not applause

Markets will always offer opportunities to earn more.

Right intention helps investors decide when **more is unnecessary**.

Wealth created without intention demands constant justification.

Wealth created with intention feels settled—even while growing.

In the long run, the most satisfied investors are not those who earned the most,

But those who knew **why they were earning at all**.

Chapter Takeaway

Wealth without intention multiplies restlessness.

Wealth with intention multiplies impact.

When the *"why"* is clear,

the *"how"* becomes calmer—and stronger.

Reflection Exercises – Chapter 16

1. **Awareness Check**

What fear or hope currently drives my financial ambition?

2. **Personal Inventory**

Which financial choices feel aligned—and which feel pressured?

3. **Behavior Mapping**

One decision I can reframe by asking: *"Why am I doing this?"*

4. **Emotional Insight**

Do comparison or purpose influence my goals more?

5. **One Quiet Commitment**

One way I will let intention—not urgency—guide my next decision.

PART - VI

Society, Economy & Compassion

EMI
EMI

Chapter - 17
Dana (Giving): The Circulation of Wealth

Why generosity strengthens abundance

How giving transforms money from possession into purpose

Why Wealth Stagnates Without Circulation

Money behaves much like energy.

When it flows with awareness, it nourishes individuals, families, and societies.

When it stagnates, fear begins to accumulate.

In Buddhist philosophy, **Dana**—the practice of giving—is not charity driven by guilt, image, or obligation. It is a conscious recognition of **interdependence**.

Dana begins with a simple understanding:

Wealth is not created in isolation.

Giving, therefore, is not loss.

It is **circulation**.

Wealth held too tightly creates anxiety—

Because what is clutched is always feared.

Wealth shared wisely creates confidence—

Because it affirms trust in continuity and sufficiency.

The Psychology behind Giving

Dana transforms the **giver** before it benefits the receiver.

Psychologically, mindful giving:

- Weakens attachment
- Reduces fear of scarcity
- Affirms a sense of "enough"
- Expands identity beyond the self

People who practice regular, intentional giving often report an unexpected outcome: **greater financial calm**.

Not because they have less money—

But because they fear loss **less**.

This is not spiritual romanticism.

It is emotional reconditioning.

Giving interrupts the belief that safety depends on accumulation alone. It trains the mind to experience stability even while letting go.

Story: Leena and the Unexpected Confidence

Leena made a simple but deliberate decision.

She began giving a small, fixed portion of her income every month. Not when she felt abundant. Not when it felt convenient. But **consistently**.

At first, anxiety surfaced.

"What if I need this later?"

"What if something goes wrong?"

Months passed.

Her finances remained stable.

But something else changed—quietly.

Leena noticed increased confidence. Money no longer felt fragile. Market fluctuations disturbed her less. Financial decisions felt calmer and clearer.

She reflected:

"Giving didn't reduce my wealth.

It reduced my fear of losing it."

Dana had not changed her income.

It had changed her **relationship with money**.

Giving Is Not Sacrifice

One of the most common misunderstandings about generosity is that it requires self-denial.

That is not Dana.

Unconscious giving—driven by guilt, pressure, or social expectation—often creates resentment.

Mindful giving creates **joy**.

True Dana is:

- Intentional
- Within capacity

- Consistent
- Free from expectation

It balances self-care with social care.

Giving that harms personal stability is not wisdom.

Giving that strengthens connection and confidence is.

Wealth as a Social Phenomenon

No wealth exists independently.

Education systems, infrastructure, stability, legal frameworks, markets, and collective trust all contribute to individual success.

Dana acknowledges this invisible support.

It reframes wealth from private accumulation to **shared resilience**.

When generosity becomes part of financial life, wealth is no longer only about security—it becomes about **participation**.

Why Giving Reduces Fear during Volatility

Fear intensifies when money feels isolated and finite.

Giving reminds the mind that:

- Resources circulate
- Support systems exist
- Life is not purely transactional

Investors who practice Dana often experience:

- Reduced panic during market downturns
- Greater emotional balance during uncertainty
- Clearer perspective on what truly matters

Generosity does not eliminate risk.

It reduces **psychological fragility**.

Practical Wisdom for Mindful Giving

Dana becomes sustainable when it is structured.

Practical guidelines include:

- Decide a **percentage**, not random amounts
- Give **regularly**, not emotionally
- Align giving with personal values
- Avoid giving from guilt or display
- Preserve personal financial stability

When giving is planned, it becomes peaceful.

When it is impulsive, it becomes draining.

Consistency matters more than scale.

Giving and Long-Term Abundance

Abundance is not only numerical.

It is emotional.

Wealth that circulates with awareness feels lighter.

Decisions become less defensive.

Goals feel less pressured.

Dana reminds investors that money is not only to be protected—but also to be **trusted**.

Investor Reflection – Chapter 17

Dana (Giving): The Circulation of Wealth

Investors often focus intensely on accumulation, while underestimating the psychological impact of circulation.

Holding wealth too tightly increases fear of loss.

Giving—when done consciously—reduces that fear.

Professionally mature investors understand a subtle truth:

Generosity is not leakage.

It is emotional risk management.

Mindful giving:

- Weakens attachment to money
- Reinforces a sense of sufficiency
- Reduces anxiety during market fluctuations

Giving also sharpens clarity.

Investors who practice Dana tend to ask better questions about:

- The purpose of wealth
- Long-term impact
- Responsibility beyond self

This does not mean giving beyond capacity or destabilizing personal finances.

It means **intentional, sustainable generosity**.

When money flows with awareness, confidence increases.

Wealth feels lighter—and decisions become calmer.

Chapter Takeaway

Money hoarded creates fear.

Money circulated creates confidence.

Giving is not about losing wealth.

It is about **belonging to life**.

Reflection Exercises – Chapter 17

1. **Awareness Check**

What emotions arise in me when I think about giving?

2. **Personal Inventory**

Does my giving feel intentional—or reactive?

3. **Behavior Mapping**

One way I can make giving regular and sustainable.

4. **Emotional Insight**

Do I give from abundance—or from obligation?

5. **One Quiet Commitment**

One act of generosity I will practice consistently.

Chapter - 18
Inequality, Consumption & Collective Karma

How individual choices shape social outcomes

Why personal financial behavior is never purely personal

When Personal Choices Become Collective Outcomes

Economic inequality is often discussed as a failure of policy, governance, or markets.

These explanations matter.

But they are incomplete.

Buddhist philosophy adds a quieter, more uncomfortable dimension: **collective karma**.

Collective karma is not destiny imposed from above.

It is not punishment.

It is not ideology.

It is the **cumulative result of millions of small, repeated individual choices**.

What we buy.

What we reward.

What we normalize.

What we ignore.

Over time, these choices solidify into systems.

Society is not something that merely happens to us.

It is an extension of our shared behavior.

Consumption Is Never Neutral

Every act of consumption sends a signal.

Not only to the market—but to society.

It signals:

- What kind of work is rewarded
- Which business models survive
- How resources are extracted or preserved
- Whose suffering remains invisible

Consumption does not end at the checkout counter.

Excessive consumption does not remain personal.

It increases pressure on resources, normalizes extraction, and widens inequality.

At the same time, deprivation for many coexists with abundance for a few—not by coincidence, but by **reinforced patterns of demand**.

Collective karma is not about blame.

It is about **shared responsibility**.

Story: Two Neighborhoods, Two Futures

Two neighborhoods developed side by side.

They had similar incomes, access to opportunity, and starting conditions.

In the first neighborhood, success was measured visibly.

- Larger homes
- Newer cars
- Frequent upgrades
- Lifestyle financed by credit
- Comparison-driven spending

In the second neighborhood, growth was quieter.

- Modest homes
- Priority given to savings
- Lower debt
- Visible community support
- Thoughtful consumption

Years passed.

The first neighborhood faced instability.

- High debt stress
- Job insecurity amplified by obligations
- Social comparison intensified anxiety
- Fragility during economic shocks

The second neighborhood developed resilience.

- Shared resources
- Lower vulnerability
- Stronger trust
- Greater capacity to absorb disruption

No ideology differed.

No policy separated them.

Behavior did.

Collective karma shaped outcomes long before any crisis arrived.

Inequality Is Amplified by Unconscious Desire

Desire itself is not harmful.

But **unconscious desire**, scaled across millions, reshapes systems.

Desire-driven systems reward:

- Speed over sustainability
- Extraction over dignity
- Growth without consequence
- Profit without responsibility

When consumption is unconscious, inequality deepens naturally.

Wealth concentrates.

Vulnerability spreads.

This is not caused by wealth itself.

It is caused by **wealth without awareness**.

Mindful wealth creation does not reject ambition.

It **integrates responsibility**.

The Buddhist Insight: Interdependence

Buddhism teaches **interdependence**.

Nothing exists independently.

No success stands alone.

Economic well-being depends on:

- Social stability
- Trust and cooperation
- Access to opportunity
- Shared dignity

Extreme inequality weakens all four.

When interdependence is ignored:

- Fear replaces trust
- Competition replaces cooperation
- Security becomes fragile
- Resentment becomes normalized

An unequal society does not fail suddenly.

It erodes quietly.

Why Inequality Eventually Affects Everyone

Inequality is often viewed as someone else's problem.

But over time, it affects:

- Market stability
- Political trust
- Social cohesion
- Long-term growth

Extreme inequality creates:

- Volatile demand
- Fragile consumer bases
- Unstable labor markets
- Rising systemic risk

From an investor's perspective, inequality is not only a moral concern.

It is a **financial risk**.

Individual Responsibility within Large Systems

You may not control global systems.

But you influence them **daily**.

Through:

- What you consume
- Where you invest
- How you earn
- Whom you support

Small actions, repeated widely, reshape norms.

Collective karma is built slowly—

But it can also be **redirected**.

Awareness changes trajectory.

Practical Ways to Act Consciously

Conscious participation does not require perfection.

It requires **attention**.

Practical steps include:

- Supporting ethical and transparent businesses
- Consuming less—but more intentionally
- Investing with awareness of long-term impact
- Giving consistently, not symbolically
- Questioning excess—even when affordable

These choices may feel small.

Together, they are **structural**.

Investor Reflection – Chapter 18

Inequality, Consumption & Collective Karma

Investors often view markets as neutral systems, separate from society.

In reality, markets are **mirrors of collective behavior**.

Every investment and consumption choice sends a signal:

- Which business models survive
- Which values are rewarded
- How resources are distributed

Unconscious consumption and purely return-driven investing can quietly contribute to inequality and systemic fragility.

Professionally thoughtful investors recognize that:

- Long-term wealth depends on social stability
- Extreme inequality weakens markets over time
- Trust and fairness are economic assets

This does not require ideological positions.

It requires **awareness**.

Investors who consider long-term impact:

- Support sustainable businesses
- Avoid extractive, short-term narratives
- Think beyond immediate profit

Collective outcomes are built slowly through repeated individual choices.

Conscious investors understand a difficult truth:

Personal wealth cannot remain secure in an unstable society.

Chapter Takeaway

Collective outcomes are not accidental.

They are rehearsed daily through personal habits.

A mindful society begins with mindful individuals.

Reflection Exercises – Chapter 18

1. Awareness Check

What kind of economy do my daily choices support?

2. Personal Inventory

Where does my comfort depend on unseen cost to others?

3. Behavior Mapping

One consumption or investment choice I can make more consciously.

4. Emotional Insight

Do fear, convenience, or comparison drive my consumption?

5. One Quiet Commitment

One small action I will repeat that supports fairness and dignity.

Chapter - 19
Wealth, Death & Impermanence

What truly remains when everything ends?

Why money finds its meaning only when time runs out

The Question We Avoid Until It Becomes Urgent

Few questions are as clarifying—and as carefully avoided—as this one:

What remains when life ends?

In Buddhist practice, reflection on death (*Maranasati*) is not morbid.

It is grounding.

Death strips life of illusion.

It removes urgency, status, and performance.

It leaves only what mattered.

Impermanence is not a future event.

It is a present condition we forget.

When wealth is examined through the lens of impermanence, its purpose becomes unmistakably clear. Money is no longer measured by how much was accumulated—but by **how wisely it supported life**.

What Wealth Can—and Cannot—Do

Seen clearly, wealth has a limited but meaningful role.

Wealth can:

- Reduce avoidable suffering
- Provide dignity, safety, and comfort
- Support education, care, and opportunity
- Create space for meaningful choices
- Enable generosity

Wealth cannot:

- Preserve identity
- Guarantee peace
- Prevent loss or grief
- Replace relationships
- Accompany us beyond life

At the end, wealth is not evaluated by size—but by **alignment**.

How it was earned.

How it was used.

How it was shared.

That is the final accounting.

Story: The Conversation That Arrived Late

An elderly man—financially successful, respected, and secure—spent his final days reflecting quietly.

There was no panic.

No complaint.

Only clarity.

When asked what he would change if given another chance, he replied:

> *"I spent too much time protecting money*
>
> *and too little time letting it support life."*

His wealth remained intact.

The moments did not.

This was not regret.

It was recognition.

Impermanence does not judge.

It **reveals.**

Impermanence as a Guide for Financial Living

When impermanence is remembered—not abstractly, but honestly—something shifts.

- Hoarding loses appeal
- Obsession weakens
- Generosity strengthens
- Priorities reorder

Ambition does not disappear.

It becomes **selective**.

You begin to ask better questions:

- Is this worth my time and attention?
- Does this purchase add meaning—or noise?
- Does this investment support life—or merely expand numbers?

Impermanence does not diminish desire.

It **refines** it.

Why We Delay Living

Many people plan responsibly for retirement—

but postpone living fully.

They delay:

- Generosity
- Rest
- Meaning
- Relationships
- Contribution

Waiting for a future that is not guaranteed.

Impermanence exposes a difficult truth:

Someday is an assumption, not a promise.

A mindful financial life does not deny the future.

It refuses to sacrifice the present entirely to it.

Legacy beyond Numbers

Legacy is often misunderstood as inheritance.

But inheritance is transfer.

Legacy is **influence**.

Legacy lives in:

- Values passed on
- Relationships preserved
- Dignity upheld
- Suffering reduced
- Courage modeled

Money can support legacy.

It cannot substitute for it.

A mindful financial life asks not only:

"How much did I accumulate?"

But:

"What did my wealth enable while I was alive?"

Living Rich, Dying Peaceful

Peace at the end of life is not created in the final year.

It is built through **years of alignment**.

A mindful approach to money prepares not just for retirement—but for closure:

- Responsibilities handled
- Relationships honored

- Generosity practiced
- Resources aligned with values

This preparation brings **lightness**, not fear.

Those who live aligned do not cling desperately at the end.

They let go naturally—because life was lived, not postponed.

Investor Reflection – Chapter 19

Wealth, Death & Impermanence

Every financial journey eventually reaches the same truth:

Wealth ends.

Meaning remains.

Investors who never reflect on impermanence often overprotect money at the cost of living well. They accumulate diligently—but postpone joy, contribution, and presence.

Professionally mature investors understand:

Money is a **means**, not an identity.

Reflection on impermanence brings clarity:

- Hoarding loses appeal
- Obsession weakens
- Priorities reorder

Wealth that is never used to support life creates regret, not security.

Those who integrate impermanence into financial thinking:

- Plan responsibly
- Give consciously
- Live fully without excess fear

The goal is not to die wealthy.

It is to **live aligned**.

Money should reduce suffering—

during life and at its end.

When this balance is achieved, wealth feels complete.

Chapter Takeaway

Wealth ends.

Meaning remains.

Those who remember impermanence

live lighter—and richer.

Reflection Exercises – Chapter 19

1. Awareness Check

If life ended today, what would truly matter to me?

2. Personal Inventory

Is my wealth serving life—or postponing it?

3. Behavior Mapping

One way I can use money to create meaning now, not later.

4. Emotional Insight

What fear or attachment makes letting go difficult?

5. One Quiet Commitment

One action I will take to align wealth with what truly lasts.

A Letter to the Indian Investor

Dear Reader,

If you have reached this point, you are not looking for shortcuts.

You are looking for something rarer:

clarity without noise,

progress without exhaustion,

wealth without inner conflict.

This letter is not advice.

It is a reflection—offered with respect.

You Live in a Time of Excess Information

Never before has so much financial information been available.

Never before have people felt so uncertain.

This contradiction is not accidental.

Information increases speed.

Wisdom requires stillness.

In your pursuit of security, growth, and responsibility, you are navigating not only markets—but expectations:

- Family expectations

- Social comparison
- Professional pressure
- Internal standards you may not have consciously chosen

Much of this pressure is invisible.

Yet it quietly shapes every decision.

This book was written to remind you of something essential:

You are allowed to slow down without falling behind.

Wealth is meant to support life — not replace it

Money is powerful.But it is not sacred.

It is a tool—for:

- Stability
- Dignity
- Choice
- Contribution

When money becomes **identity**, fear enters.

When money becomes **responsibility**, clarity returns.

You do not need to optimize every decision.

You need to **align enough decisions consistently**.

Quiet consistency outperforms constant intensity.

You Will Never Eliminate Uncertainty — And That Is Okay

Markets will fluctuate.

Careers will evolve.

Plans will change.

The goal was never certainty.The goal is **resilience**.

Preparation matters more than prediction.

Behavior matters more than brilliance.

Patience matters more than urgency.

If this book has given you:

- One pause before reacting,
- One moment of awareness before deciding,
- One reminder to choose balance over extremes,

Then it has already served its purpose.

A Quiet Truth from Experience

After decades of observing people and markets, one pattern remains constant:

Those who grow wealth **peacefully** rarely talk about it.

They focus on:

- Consistency
- Ethics
- Patience
- Long horizons

- Inner stability

They are not immune to doubt.They simply refuse to let doubt **drive**.

Wherever You Are — You Are Not Late

If you are early in your journey: build habits patiently.

If you are mid-way: protect what you have built.

If you are successful: use wealth to reduce suffering—yours and others.'

If you are uncertain: remember that clarity arrives faster through **stillness** than urgency.

There is no single correct pace.There is only **conscious direction**.

A Final Thought

One day, markets will no longer matter to you.

But how you lived will.

May your money serve your life.

May your wealth feel light.

May your decisions bring calm—not noise.

And may you walk the **Middle Path**,

not because it is easy,

but because it **endures**.

With respect,

— Ram Gaikwad

Author

Conclusion – A Mindful Financial Life

Where wealth ends, and wisdom begins

This book began with a simple but uncomfortable question:

Why does money—meant to support life—so often disturb it?

As the pages unfolded, one truth became steadily clearer.

The problem was never money.

It was never markets.

It was never returns.

It was the **mind**.

Money does not create anxiety, greed, fear, or restlessness.

It **reveals** them.

It amplifies whatever remains unexamined within us.

Through the lens of Buddhist wisdom—balance, awareness, patience, compassion, non-attachment—we discovered that financial struggle is rarely about intelligence or income. It is about relationship.

Our relationship with:

- Desire
- Uncertainty
- Time
- Control
- Enough
- Impermanence

A mindful financial life does not reject ambition.

It refines it.

It does not escape modern finance.

It **humanizes** it.

From Accumulation to Alignment

Modern culture teaches us to accumulate first and ask questions later.

This book suggested the opposite.

When intention is clear, accumulation becomes purposeful.

When awareness is present, discipline becomes natural.

When patience is practiced, compounding works quietly.

When attachment loosens, anxiety softens.

When generosity flows, abundance feels lighter.

A mindful investor is not passive.

They are **anchored**.

They understand:

- Markets fluctuate
- Outcomes vary
- Life interrupts plans

And yet, they remain steady—not because they control the future, but because they have learned to relate wisely to uncertainty.

What This Book Ultimately Asks

This book does not ask you to abandon wealth.

It asks you to **use it consciously**.

It does not ask you to fear desire.

It asks you to **understand it**.

It does not ask you to reject success.

It asks you to **define it honestly**.

And finally, it asks a question most financial books avoid:

When everything ends,

will your money have supported your life—

or postponed it?

The Quiet Achievement

A mindful financial life may not look dramatic.

It is often quiet.

- Fewer emotional decisions
- Fewer regrets
- Fewer desperate reactions

But its outcomes are profound:

- Calm during volatility
- Clarity during choice
- Dignity during uncertainty
- Peace during closure

This is not the absence of ambition.

It is ambition **without inner violence**.

A Final Reflection

One day, markets will no longer matter to you.

Numbers will stop updating.

Accounts will be closed.

What will remain is simpler—and more important:

- How you lived
- How you treated others
- How you related to fear and desire
- How lightly or heavily you carried wealth

A mindful life prepares not only for retirement,

but for **completion**.

A Blessing, Not a Promise

May your wealth grow **responsibly**.

May your mind grow **freely**.

May your ambition remain **grounded**.

May your generosity remain **alive**.

And may your life feel **complete**—

long before the end arrives.

30 Quotes for 30 Days

(Original, inspired by Buddhist wisdom & the book's philosophy)

1. Wealth grows faster when desire is disciplined and slower when it is ignored.
2. Money reveals the mind long before it rewards intelligence.
3. The problem is not uncertainty—it is our refusal to accept it.
4. Enough is not a number; it is a state of clarity.
5. What you repeat with money becomes your character.
6. Patience is not waiting—it is staying.
7. Markets test knowledge; life tests balance.
8. Saving is not fear of tomorrow—it is care for it.
9. Debt steals freedom quietly, one commitment at a time.
10. Greed promises speed but delivers regret.
11. Fear protects from loss—but also from growth.
12. True financial strength is the ability to remain calm under fluctuation.

13. Contentment is invisible wealth that protects visible wealth.

14. When money becomes identity, peace becomes fragile.

15. Ethics may slow earnings—but they accelerate trust.

16. You don't lose peace because of markets; you lose it because of attachment.

17. Wealth without awareness amplifies anxiety.

18. The best investment is emotional discipline.

19. What feels urgent is rarely important.

20. Generosity reduces fear more than accumulation ever can.

21. Money managed without balance demands attention; money managed wisely gives it back.

22. Success earned in silence lasts longer than success announced loudly.

23. Impermanence is not a threat—it is a reminder to prepare wisely.

24. The market rewards those who endure boredom more than those who chase excitement.

25. Desire moves the finish line; contentment allows arrival.

26. Wealth is meant to support life, not replace it.

27. Every financial decision trains the mind—choose carefully what you repeat.

28. Peace is not found after achieving more, but after needing less.

29. True freedom is uncommitted time, unburdened income, and an unattached mind.

30. When the end arrives, meaning remains—numbers do not.